Quick-Start Writing Guide for Graduate Research and Writing

Quick-Start Writing Guide for Graduate Research and Writing

Susan Smith Nash, Ph.D.

tP
Texture Press
2016

Texture Press
1108 Westbrooke Terrace
Norman, OK 73072
www.texturepress.org

Executive Editor: Susan Smith Nash, Ph.D.
Associate Editor: Valerie Fox, Ph.D.
Publicity / Public Relations Manager: Arlene Ang

For ordering information,
please visit the Texture Press website at
www.texturepress.org

ISBN-13: 978-1-945784-03-3
ISBN-10: 1-945784-03-2

Book design by Arlene Ang

This work is licensed under the Creative Commons Attribution-NoDerivatives 4.0 International License. To view a copy of this license, visit http://creativecommons.org/licenses/by-nd/4.0/ or send a letter to Creative Commons, PO Box 1866, Mountain View, CA 94042, USA.

• TABLE OF CONTENTS •

Quick-Start Guide Writing Guide for Graduate Research and Writing 7
Initial Considerations 16
Getting Started with Discovery Writing 19
Composition Invention Strategies: Power for the Paper You Must Write 22
Pit Bull Brainstorming: Invention Strategies for Composition 28
Rubrics as Full-Process Compositional Power Tools 32
Plagiarism: Risky Swimming 36
Worksheet: Vivid Writing 38
One-Stop Shopping for Expository Essays 41
Writing for Business with a Tourism / Hospitality Focus 49
Process Writing: The Instruction Sheet 50
Proposal 53
Example of Developing a Proposal 55
Using Flowcharts to Respond to Writing Assignments 59
Writing to Explore an Ethical Dilemma: A Mini-Essay 65
Current Problem / Analysis Paper 67
The Research Process 77
Research Paper Survival Guide & Flowchart 80
Research Paper Getting Started Freewrite 82
Research Paper Overview 84
Revising Your Paper 90
Writing Literature Reviews 92
Structure of the Annotated Bibliography Literature Review 94

Literature Review Topic Selection	97
Literature Review: Planning Worksheet	99
Literature Review: Single Annotated Bibliography	101
Example of the Annotated Bibliography for a Single Source	104
Literature Review: Multi-Article/Reference Annotated Bibliographies	107
Literature Review: In-Text Citations	109
Argumentation in Action: The Debate	111
Capstone, Thesis, or Term Paper Guide	117
Literary Narrative: Discovery Moment! Worksheet	120
Worksheet 2: Cultural Heritage and Human Relations	137
Writing For Self-Discovery, Revisited	140
Autobiographical Moments: My Leadership Moments	144
Prompt: When did I have to reinvent myself? How did I do it?	145
Prompt: When was a time I overcame the discomfort I felt upon being far outside my comfort zone?	148
Telling Your Story: Getting Started	150
Telling the Story of Your Life	152
Prompt: Creativity	157
Prompt: Freewrite	161
Example: Journey	165
Boom And Bust	170
Appendix: Example of a Research Paper in Progress	172
About the Author	187

Quick-Start Guide Writing Guide for Graduate Research and Writing

I'm in Graduate School now, but can I write well enough to survive?

If you're waking up in the middle of the night and wondering if your academic writing skills are sufficient to carry you successfully through graduate school, you're not alone.

And, to be honest, you have reason to worry.

The expectations in graduate school are significantly higher than in undergraduate programs, especially if you were in a degree program that did not require very many term papers, article evaluations from your research, or presentations.

The truth of the matter is that a perfectly undergraduate acceptable essay that describes a concept or phenomenon probably will not be rigorous enough in graduate school. Further, it will not demonstrate the kinds of questions you need to ask, or the depth of critical thinking that you need to demonstrate. Further, your evidence (especially the facts, figures, and expert views) that you need to provide, is likely to be inadequate.

How do you prepare yourself to succeed in graduate school? What are the things you need to be sure to demonstrate in your academic writing?

You're in luck. Help is here.

Welcome to a guide to graduate-level writing, which contains the material you'll need, in the order that will be most useful to you.

First, you'll have a quick checklist that you can apply to all your graduate-level academic writing.

Second, you'll have a handy overview of graduate writing "how-to" which will help you quickly achieve the levels of competency you need to have in order to not just pass courses, but succeed with good grades.

Finally, there are flowcharts, examples, and activities—all of which will help you become a writer with great skills and self-knowledge—a powerful (and potentially unstoppable) combination.

Getting Started: Your Professor Is Not a Killer Cat

You've probably heard of the National Geographic experiment (and then memorialized by The Oatmeal—http://theoatmeal.com/comics/cats_actually_kill) where cats were outfitted with mini-cams in order to see what they were actually up to when they roamed around in the wild, rather than sticking with the confining role of "house kitty." The kitty-cams revealed that free-range cats kill once every few days, and they kill, not for hunger, but for the pure thrill of the kill.

Now that you're in graduate school, there is probably a sneaking suspicion that your professors are like those free range "killer kitties" who like nothing more than to wound, maim, and kill the little neighborhood lizards and innocent little voles, just for the sense of a successful hunt, and to "gift" them to their department chair or the provost.

And, what is the "killer kitties" secret weapon? You guessed it! The writing assignment, whether it be term paper, a study in depth, a presentation, or a thesis or comprehensive exam, seems to be the weapon of choice.

Rejoice! Reality Check. Professors are NOT "Killer Kitties" and they actually want to help you succeed!

So, help is here. This guide will help you succeed in graduate writing activities, and further, will help you improve each time you complete a writing assignment for a course.

Let's start with the basics: To write well, you must think well.

Although many students would prefer to think of good writing as something innate—or, better, as bad writing as something they have been inoculated against—the reality is that writing is a skill developed over time.

Writing is not simply a series of talented moves or gestures. To write well requires one to think well. The writer must organize his or her argument and, on a more fundamental level, he or she must be able to simultaneously consider all the factors that go into constructing a good essay, report, article, or paper. Not only does the learner need to be able to analyze and organize facts and figures, he or she must also consider the purpose of the activity.

Some of the questions that should be invoked include the following: What is the ultimate aim? Who is the intended audience, and what characteristics to they have? In addition the writer must envision the writing task from the point of view of the author's motives, the audience, and social context. Further, in a larger frame, it is important to understand what is often referred to as the "rhetorical situation," a term first coined by Lloyd Bitzer, a professor of rhetoric whose research interests focused on strategies used in persuasive discourse and the construction of effective arguments. According to Bitzer, a rhetorical situation occurs when an author, audience, and a social context converge to create a rhetorical act, such as an act of writing or speaking.

The rhetorical situation is commonly depicted in the rhetorical triangle. The discourse that is being produced is considered the "medium," because it is through this that the author, audience, and social context come together, each with a potentially mediating influence. In this case, "mediation" refers to the power it exerts to subtly change or overtly co-opt meaning.

Please keep in mind that the rhetorical triangle changes shape depending upon the kind of discourse being produced. For example, academic writing will be depicted in a different way than advertising.

In the 1970s and 80s, numerous articles were written about the "rhetorical situation," and it achieved almost mythical status in terms of its efficacy to explain how the dynamics of persuasion work in the phenomenal world. The discussions were expanded with the notions of Jacques Derrida, who, with the concept of "differance," (discussed in his 1981 essay, "Semiology and Grammatology") interjects the interplay of psychology and social context, to demonstrate how internalized notions of authority further exert influence on how meaning(s) are generated. Foregrounding the act of interpretation, either conscious or unconscious, Derrida emphasizes that there are numerous factors that bear upon how the idea of the humanistic subject comes into being. That subject becomes deconstructed once its ontological pillars are undermined, and as Derrida points out, there are many ways to collapse those ontological moorings.

With the approach of "differance" in mind, as texts are produced and interpreted, it is useful to look at the activities that take place on the edges of the rhetorical triangle, and how relationships are forged. For example, the notion of identity is destabilized once we realize how it is not an absolute, but it protean, metamorphosing element, which changes in response to dreams or fantasies, social pressure, which can create tensions between the ideal and the real, the flawed original and its perfect simulacra. The subject, which in this case, would be writing and speech, are likewise destabilized by "differance."

In 2004, with e-mail, the Internet, text-messaging via PDAs and cell phones, the model continues to be useful. What tends to add variables are sub-categories of context and author. For example, the context may be synchronous, asynchronous, or a combination of both. What this means is that the realm of academic writing has expanded and that it is more vital than ever for the writer to understand the conventions of the particular genre or occasion, and how they shape reader expectations.

Writing for college is a fairly complex task and the conventions are not always expressed as clearly as one might hope. For that reason, it is vital for a learner to have taken at least one course that focuses exclusively on academic writing. This will form the core for skills, knowledge, and analytical thinking which will be expanded and built upon as the student progresses. Although there is wide latitude in the degree of formality found in writing for college, the boundaries for a particular writing occasion can be very narrowly constrained. This can cause frustration for the learner who has not acquired the conceptual, analytical, or problem-solving skills to able to successfully negotiate the situation.

That said, there is no reason to fear academic writing. The same basic building blocks reappear in many places and are applied in many situations, with modifications made in accordance with the writing occasion.

For example, the basic building block, the paragraph, is used not only in constructing essays and research papers, but is also required in essay exams that require expository writing. The ability to shape an argument: present a clear thesis statement, with supporting evidence requires processing and understanding the system of logic that underpins the argument.

Writing for college may seem a bit daunting at first, but ultimately it is one of the most satisfying experiences one can have. Not only is it a self-esteem builder to be able to structure an argument, it is deeply affirming to be able to communicate with others who have similar goals and interests, that is to say an affinity group.

In addition to writing essays for example and communicating with other learners, it is also important to be able to successfully produce academic essays. There are a number of genres or "modes" to manage. These are either presented as stand-alone essays or they constitute components of a larger work, such as a research paper, thesis, or dissertation. The forms most frequently encountered in academic writing are the following:

Extended Definition: In addition to definitions and descriptions of the thing under consideration, this essay explores how it is that we know. Evidence is critical, as well as clear sentences. Although essays are often "stand-alones," many times this is section of a larger paper.

Chronological Narrative: While creative non-fiction utilizes this mode in the construction of memoirs or histories, it is also important to be able to write this type of essay. These are used in histories (in history, international relations, political science, sociology), as well as in presenting biographical background and a notion of the provenance and evolution of an idea within a research paper or thesis.

Compare-Contrast Essay: While it is hard to imagine a research paper or thesis centered on comparison-contrast, the ability to write a well-formed essay is important, particularly for essay tests.

Taking a Position: One can argue that all expository writing is a variation of this, or at least incorporates some of the structure. Argumentation and persuasive writing involve careful planning, not only in gathering research, but also in bringing together evidence and constructing the logic that will help support one's position.

Process: This is an essay which includes how to do something or tell how something happens. It is very important for individuals who will take technical writing courses.

Cause and Effect: Cause and effect essays are widely-found, and they provide an excellent opportunity to look for logical fallacies and inadequate evidence.

Here it is useful to emphasize again that there exists a close connection between writing and thinking. To write well requires one to be able to think flexibly and about the various aspects of the rhetorical triangle. The more cynical writer may dismiss this as a call to generate clichés, and that academic writing merely asks the student to subjugate individual difference in order to conform to a rigid pattern. This is most often presented as an objection when students are asked to submit their writing to automated grading systems such as MyAccess.com, or when they are writing for a standardized test such as the SAT that utilizes similar artificial intelligence-fired programs.

However, instead of generating clichés, writing in a mode or genre can be profoundly stimulating, even liberating, inasmuch as it allows self-expression and the construction of possibility, new ways of looking at, perceiving, or conceptualizing the world.

Much, of course, depends on the rhetorical situation. This means considering all the factors mentioned earlier, and more. The following questions resurface, but rephrased in ways that allow conscious deconstruction of the argument, subjectivity, and relationships between the sides of the rhetorical triangle: Why did the author write the piece? What were the conditions under which it was produced? What was the context? What was the goal of the writer vis-à-vis the readers? How was language employed? How is the writing intended to function within the world? What are the assumptions and beliefs of the audience? How does the social context in which it is read and produced influence the production and interpretation of the text?

To appreciate this task, the learner must learn how to conduct what is often referred to as a "close reading" of the text. This does not mean simply capturing the denotative content of the argument, but instead, requires readers to become active interrogators, and to be able to ask questions that begin to reveal the issues surrounding the rhetorical triangle: intended audience, perceived social context, conditions under which one anticipates the text will be read.

At the same time, such questioning will also begin to allow elements to surface, even though they may begin as disguised or submerged. For example, underlying assumptions within the argument that include beliefs, ontological positions with respect to the validity of "evidence," cultural constructions, notions about how it is that we know (tests of the "real"), and when and how something is considered to have meaning, and/or be meaningful. However abstruse or perversely recondite these concepts seem at first encounter, it is definitely worthwhile to go to the effort to understand them and their implications. Awareness, self-consciousness, an ability to construct effective questions, and highly-evolved analytical skills are as vital for learners in college courses as for instructors, guides, and general inhabitants of the planet.

Recently, literary analysis, close reading, and the writing process have begun to preoccupy themselves with understanding how it is that learners become motivated to write essays. Instead of looking only at form and engaging in a close reading of the text(s), there has been a fervent focus on "situated learning," and "embodied experience." First developed by J. Lave in 1998, the concept of "situated learning" suggests that "learning as it normally occurs is a function of the activity, context and culture in which it occurs (i.e. it is situated)" (Lave 192) and "contrasts with traditional classroom learning activities which involve knowledge which is often presented in an abstract form and out of context" (Lave 193).

Thus, to be most effective, it is important to structure activities so that they have a grounding in something that is perceived as ontologically tangible. That can be a person's experience, current events, current perceptions and beliefs, or a set of activities centered on a community of practice. "Anchored instruction" occurs in a setting when an instructor deliberately "anchors" or "situates" the activity. It follows, then, that college writing learning and teaching activities should be designed around a 'anchor' (or situation) which could be some sort of case-study or problem situation. In preparing for the writing activity, the readings, discussion materials, settings to analyze should allow exploration within the essay or text produced.

By establishing a point of contact, the activities are perceived as relevant to one's life, and also useful in helping explain the world at large. The motivating aspects of this cannot be overstated. Instead of simply checking a box and satisfying a requirement, the students find that their activities help them untangle and understand their world. It invokes Kenneth Burke's notion that literature (and by extension, writing) is "equipment for living."

Initial Considerations

Let's take a brief initial look at three critical areas:

>Plagiarism
>Citing Sources
>Databases and reliable sources

We're introducing the topics now, but will go in depth later in the text.

Plagiarism: The Zombie that Will Eat Your Brain.

As repellent as it is, this is a subject can't be avoided. Academic dishonesty will destroy you. So, learn how to write and cite correctly, and produce papers that incorporate YOUR ideas, and at the same time, showcase YOUR intellectual acumen.

Plagiarism is a zombie that will eat your brain. Other people's thoughts and ideas will supplant your own. Before you know it, you are not even YOU any more, and you are harnessed to the words, ideas, and impulses that come from the general zeitgeist, and, ultimately, make no sense at all, except to destroy you.

Plagiarism Has Many Forms

>Copying and Pasting from the Internet
>Passing off someone else's work as your own
>Passing off work from another course as "fresh" for another
>Using the ideas of others without referencing them (in-text citation is best)
>Creating Patchwork Quilt of Block Quotations: Losing the "You" in the Quilt
>Paraphrasing without Attribution
>Summarizing without Attribution

Citing Sources Properly
The American Psychological Association is the citation style that you should use for the social sciences. Be sure to follow the style guide very carefully. First and foremost, you need to have the APA cite bookmarked as a "favorite" on your laptop or phone. You may wish to use the Purdue OWL's website, which is very convenient: https://owl.english.purdue.edu/owl/resource/560/01/)

Getting to know databases.

Online databases are absolutely indispensable. Here are a few useful ones:

Government statistics
FedStats: Gateway to statistics from more than 100 agencies
    https://fedstats.sites.usa.gov/
ChildStats: Child and Family Statistics.
    http://www.childstats.gov/

World Bank and United Nations free sources
The World Bank Open Knowledge Repository:
    https://openknowledge.worldbank.org/
UNData: United Nations Data http://data.un.org/Default.aspx

Databases with articles and full-text monographs:
Business Source Premier
EBSCO host
JStor
Project Muse
Proquest
PsycARTICLES
Social Theory
SocINDEX
The SAGE Handbook of Mental Health and Illness
Wall Street Journal Historical Newspaper
Women and Social Movements in the United States

New York Public Library

http://digitalcollections.nypl.org/

Library of Congress
https://www.loc.gov/

Directory of Open Access Journals
https://doaj.org/

Elsevier Open Access
https://www.elsevier.com/about/open-science/open-access/open-access-journals

Free Open Access Online Articles (highwire)
http://highwire.stanford.edu/lists/freeart.dtl

Getting Started with Discovery Writing

Getting to know yourself and your values is one of the many benefits of "discovery writing." Be looking within yourself and analyzing your responses to the things that happen in your life and in the world around you, you'll have a chance to write with more self-awareness and potential objectivity.

The process of writing allows you to
- Organize your thoughts
- Sort out your feelings
- Evaluate evidence
- Construct a reality of your own, and compare it with the realities that other have
- Create lists
- Uncover your own ideas / feelings
- Develop explanations and meaningful connections

Because one may have extremely lofty goals when starting to write, it's often easy to become completely blocked or paralyzed.

One effective way to break through writer's block is to shape your thoughts in the form of a brief autobiographical "self-discovery writing." Here are examples:

Discovery Writing #1:

Write a very brief one-paragraph response to each of the prompts. The responses should flow from free-writes and should be very informal, since the purpose is to explore and brainstorm. The paragraphs should be very brief—2 or 3 sentences per paragraph is fine.

Who Am I? What Are My Roots? Where Did My Beliefs (even the ones I'm uncomfortable with) Come from? Part of being able to relate to a problem or to other people involves

understanding yourself. Here is a good opportunity to discover how you perceive your own history.
- An early memory "flash memory"
- My father's characteristic behaviors
- My mother's characteristic behaviors
- A typical family (or lonely) activity
- A book, television show, popular song (or group), or movie from your childhood

Discovery Writing #2:

Write a very brief one-paragraph response to each of the prompts. The responses should flow from free-writes and should be very informal, since the purpose is to explore and brainstorm. The paragraphs should be very brief—2 or 3 sentences per paragraph is fine.

Challenging Moments. We are often faced with ethical choices when we encounter challenges. What do we do? Do we behave ethically? Do we consider human dignity, respect, and the rights of all involved?
- A time in my life I was faced with a challenge I had to overcome
- A time I observed something unethical
- A time I felt proud of doing the right thing
- A time I was not sure what to do—and still am not quite sure…
- Stranger in a strange land—or feeling totally lost, unmoored

Discovery Writing #3:

Write a very brief one-paragraph response to each of the prompts. The responses should flow from free-writes and should be very informal, since the purpose is to explore and brainstorm. The paragraphs should be very brief—2 or 3 sentences per paragraph is fine.

Things that make me smile, things that motivate me (sometimes it's good to realize that ethical behavior ties closely to you care about and what motivates you.

- Small pleasures
- Naughty Dog! How I love my pet(s)!
- Things of beauty
- Connecting to nature
- New experiences, new cultures

Where do you store your memories?

Composition Invention Strategies:
Power for the Paper You Must Write

There are many ways to kick off the writing process. Some of the best approaches involve simply listing ideas or freewriting without any kind of censoring or restrictive thought. The key is to start the flow of ideas and to discover everything you can about what you want to learn about the topic, what you want your audience to do, what kind of discursive outcome (rhetorical situation) do you think you'll be able to accomplish, and what uncovered (and creative) connections there may be.

Key elements:

- flow of ideas
- topic discovery
- audience persuasion / "do" something
- ultimate outcome
- unique and undiscovered connections

Techniques

There are many effective techniques in the "getting started" phase. It is often a good idea to try more than one when writing.

Topic bulls-eye:

This is a great way to narrow your topic. Write down the first main idea or topic that comes to mind. Then, consider the topic and whether or not it is too narrow or too broad. Write down other terms or words that approximate or approach the main idea. Soon, you'll start honing in on the topic that makes the most sense, given your goals.

Goals Description and Your Own Personal "Rhetorical Situation":

What do you want your paper to do? Lloyd Bitzer wrote of "the rhetorical situation" in his now classic article (yes, please Google it now. It will do you good. I can provide a link but you're better off looking it up yourself, and then thinking about how it ties to your own prior knowledge). The "rhetorical situation" is something I like to refer to as the "persuasion equation." It's the end-product and result of the actions and activities.

For example, if you want your piece of discourse to persuade a group of people to vote for a certain candidate, you'll approach your writing activity much differently than if you want to persuade someone to purchase a new smoothie at a local organic grocery store. You'll need to know something about your audience, their values, their goals, the context, and competing ideas or "rhetors."

But, before we get too complicated or digress into some of the outer reaches of the "rhetorical situation," let's step back and break it down. To get started, we need to simply look at our goals and objectives. What do we want to accomplish? Here's where bullet points can be useful.

Quick-list of goals:

- audience attitudes to change
- audience actions to inspire
- values and emotions to incorporate
- author reputation to shore up

Uncensored Freewrite: The Deep Dive Into Your Unconscious
Can you write for 5 minutes without stopping? You might be surprised how difficult it is to do. Sometimes it's almost impossible if you're easily distracted by social media or the Internet. And, sometimes, you have to trick yourself and put your freewrite in a form that simulates a situation you care about. For example, you may need to create a situation in which you're writing a letter to someone about a situation you care about. Or, you may need to pretend your writing in your journal about things that you observed

but that bothered you, or which triggered emotions.

Of course, this is probably the most difficult of all things to do—after all, we spend much of our lives trying to avoid emotions or at least to channel them. Self-control is a good thing, but sometimes it keeps us from really understanding ourselves, and it pushes us into a rut of predictable, proscribed responses.

If you have committed yourself to a freewrite, be sure to tell yourself that you do not have to show it to anyone, and also that grammatical errors, spelling, facts, etc. are not as important as you might think they are. They can always be revised later. What you're trying to accomplish right now is a deep dive into your unconscious.

MindMaps: Triggering connections through graphical representation.

There are a number of tools that can help you if you prefer computer graphics to a pen and piece of paper in which you write words, and then associated ideas or concepts which you then branch out. The mindmap helps you visually see the way you relate your concepts or ideas, and the visual representation triggers more thoughts and ideas. After you complete the mindmap you can save it, or use it after you've completed your first draft in order to identify where you have gaps or unexplored connection.

Here's a free mindmap program (http://drichard.org/mindmaps/) which does not have all the functionality of a MindMeister (or your own piece of paper and pen), but it's a great way to get started. If you don't need all the functionality, you can always simply use Google Slides or PowerPoint to start some ideas and then share with your collaborators to start creating interactive brainstorming.

Here's an example just using a word processing program (Okay, MS-Word):

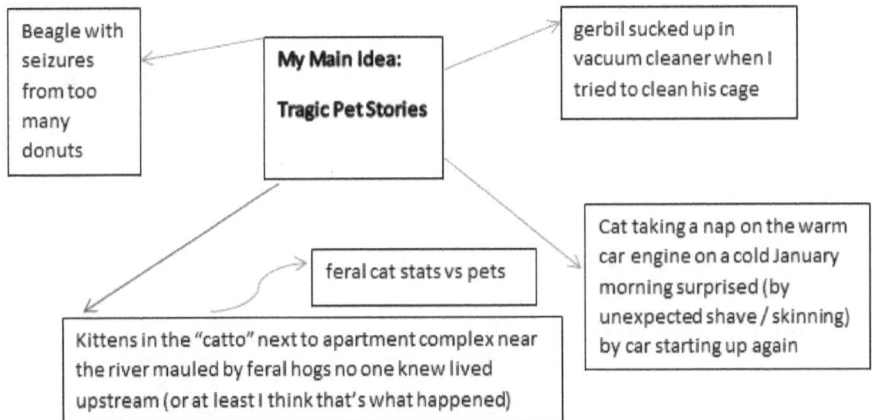

Gamification as Invention Strategy in Writing Essays and Research Papers

Using games can be a good way to get your mind moving. Now you ask: What kind of games? It could be something where you have to search for something, but the quest approach sometimes does not yield what you need, which is a well-developed idea of the topic in which you are immersed to the point that you basically become the problem. What we're describing is, as you can already see, a role-playing game.

So, the very first step in gamification for brainstorming is to identify a problem.

What would Halo 5's Master Chief Petty Officer John-117 do?

What would The Joker do?

Next, start clarifying the mission and the characters for role-playing.

- My Challenge: Dealing with escaped exotic pets in my neighborhood
- Role Play: What would my favorite game character do?
- Role Play, Second Round: What would a famous videogame villain or bad guy do? (What would Bowser do? What would

The Joker do?)

Now, once you've set up your scenario, don't let a lack of in-depth knowledge about your selected heroes or anti-heroes slow you down. Remember, your goal is to think of solving a problem, and how to do it in an expedient way that may or may not be very ethical. If you are the extremely unethical Joker, then be sure to reflect on how and why your choices are so, well, evil.

Keep in mind that the gamified mind is the following:

- Mission-focused
- Aware of causal relationships / cause & effect
- Very aware of surroundings
- Able to predict obstacles and anticipate likely dangers
- Very aware of competitors and impediments
- Focused on winning / the prize (desired outcome)
- Ready to maximize efficiency step by step
- Willing to apply knowledge gained by prior experience
- Able to quickly search for helpful information when needed

Gamifying your mind can be a powerful approach to brainstorming because it helps you overcome some of the blocks you might have when you try to develop an idea using written text and outlines, where you are staying perhaps too abstract and conceptual. By adding the gaming approach, you're involved in a simulation, and thus are engaging on a higher plane where you are a whole person, focused on an outcome. Focusing on an outcome allows you to organize, streamline, and reality-check your approach, and it forces you to become creative if you see certain obstacles or dangers. By role-playing both a hero and a villain, you're able to evaluate ethical and unethical choices.

When might gamification not work? It's possible to completely stall out on gamification if

- your goal is not challenging enough
- your goal can't be defined

- you can't identify any obstacles
- there are no ethical challenges

If you're stalling out, you may need to revisit your topic and consider how to make it more complex, so that you have more room to expand your thought process.

After you've completed your gamification scenario, the next step is to take a look at transforming the scenario into an outline. You'll start with THE PROBLEM, and the move to SOLUTIONS, which will be your outline.

Pit Bull Brainstorming:
Invention Strategies for Composition

Brainstorming is an invention strategy for composition that can take many forms. While some find it useful to use diagrams, outlines, decision trees, and clusters, those tactics tend to focus on the "what" instead of the "how" and the "why." In order to approach deeper issues, and to trigger chains of thoughts, a very powerful technique is to develop series of questions.

This brainstorming exercise revolves around questions that trigger questions. It is a chain of questions, or, one could say a "great concatenation of questions." This approach is extremely useful for causal essays, as well as basic argumentation. One topic that certainly helps illustrate the technique is that of the American Pit Bull Terrier. It seems that attacks by pit bulls just keep increasing. Why is it happening? What are we doing about it? Are some dog breeds being labeled "bad breeds"?

I'm using the question about whether or not communities should have "breed bans" as an example. Use this approach for any topic—you'll be surprised how effect it is, especially as you try to get started, and you are not sure how to see multiple sides of the same issue.

Getting Started: What's the provocative topic? Ban the Breed! (but does it really work? Is it fair?)

Dog attacks are often attributed to specific breeds, deemed by the public to be "vicious" or bloodthirsty. But what is behind this?

Where can I find a clear overview of the issue?

The ASPCA has dedicated a web page to the issues surrounding "Breed-Specific Legislation." In their view, "Breed-Specific" laws

are discriminatory:
http://www.aspca.org/animal-cruelty/dog-fighting/what-breed-specific-legislation

The ASPA has issued a detailed position paper on Breed-Specific Legislation. It is illuminating on many levels:
http://www.aspca.org/about-us/aspca-policy-and-position-statements/position-statement-breed-specific-legislation

The "Concatenation of Questions": Questions immediately came to mind. I thought about the general questions, and I found my questions were helping me narrow my topic.
The questions can also be thought of as cluster analysis questions, and can be used in conjunction with mind-mapping.
The perplexing questions first:

- Why do pit pulls attack people, and how can such a tiny dog be so dangerous?
- Who says they're bad? Why are they saying it?
- What do some people want to do? Where? Why?
- What are the unintended consequences of blanket-banning a breed (such as pit bulls)?
- Do the dogs suffer? When and how?
- Do the owners suffer? When and how?
- What's the impact on public safety? (any "backfire" issues? Consequences? (romanticizing "outlaws" and "outlaw breeds"?)

History and background thoughts:
- Why are pit bulls aggressive? Were they bred that way?
- What is a pit bull, and what makes it so dangerous?
- Who uses the ultra-aggressive pit bulls?
- Who might need such an aggressive dog?

The other side of the coin:
- What is good about a pit bull?
- Why do some people say the breed is very loving?

- Can pit bulls be friendly, happy dogs?

Let's get personal:
- What would I do if I had a pit bull?
- Training, conditioning, behavior modification
- Are there any business opportunities here? Yes! one can specialize in deprogramming dangerous dogs; also, let your city become the pit bull dumping ground next to a major metropolitan area (all dogs must be muzzled, though)
- Dog chow for ultra aggressive dogs (make them more aggressive)—is there and ethical issue here?
- Pacifying dog chow (calm down and tranquilize the dogs)
-

Starting (& Ending) With Questions

What do we see from different perspectives?

What gives us confidence to tackle what seems potentially overwhelming?

Pit Bulls and Dog Fighting: Current Issues

Dog Fighting: The Criminal, Underground World of Dog Fighting: http://www.aspca.org/animal-cruelty/dog-fighting

PETA and Dogfighting: http://www.peta.org/issues/animals-in-entertainment/cruel-sports/dogfighting/

64 Pit Bulls Seized in Major Dog Fighting Raid in Illinois: http://www.inquisitr.com/3020899/64-pit-bulls-seized-in-major-dog-fighting-raid-in-illinois/

Dog Fighting Ring Busted in Linda Vista:
http://fox5sandiego.com/2016/03/30/9-pit-bulls-found-in-san-diego-la-dog-fighting-ring/

My Pit Bull Brainstorming "cloud"—make connections

Pit bull terriers, composition strategies, animal cruelty, dog fighting, "outlaw" dogs, discrimination, brainstorming techniques, concept mapping, clusters of thoughts, invention techniques, first year composition, mad dog, mauling dogs, 76-year-old-woman mauled by pit bull as grandchildren watch in horror, Denver bans pit bulls, Nederland, Colorado becomes aggressive breed haven, new kennel accepts cast-off killer canines

Narrowing with More Questions:

- What are the ethical issues of breed bans?
- How might breed bans help or harm the quest to eradicate animal cruelty (specifically dog fighting)?
- Any unintended consequences?
- What is the impact of an economic downturn on breed bans?

Rubrics as Full-Process Compositional Power Tools

Start, rather than end, with the rubric?
A rubric can be used in the invention phase of writing, not just in assessments. It is just a matter of perspective, and whether or not you're willing to create a rubric that piques the imagination and triggers a series of ideas of how to structure and build the essay or other piece of discourse.

The ideal rubric can be both a "triggering rubric" and a "checklist rubric" and can be used in the invention, outlining, drafting, and revision phases of writing. Here are the uses of a good rubric:

1. Brainstorming / invention: Reading the rubric can trigger thoughts and ideas, and help with narrowing / focusing the main idea and clarifying the desired outcome or goal of the writing
2. Outlining: Developing an appropriate sequence, as well as connections back to the main idea and the writing purpose or goal
3. Drafting: Thinking of the best possible examples and supporting evidence, deciding where to place statistics, examples, case studies, and references to published reports
4. Revising: Triggering thoughts and ideas about where there might be gaps and a need for expansion, and also where it might be necessary to cut, prune, or reorganize

Customized Rubrics: Reinforce mission, passion, vision, and the "rhetorical situation"

Working with a rubric does not have to be a dry, boring experience. Yes, it can certainly be used to check boxes and to carefully assess whether or not a paper has met expectations at each level of competency.
For example, you can use your rubric to incorporate additional criteria besides the typical "purpose statement" and "organization." You can add rows for additional criteria:

1. Reflects ethical values, respect for diversity, and a sense of fair play
2. Demonstrates competency in the technical area in the topic
3. Exhibits rigorous research design and method
4. Discusses competing perspectives or views in a thorough-going manner
5. Uses several types of supporting evidence, which can include statistics, case studies, examples, and research study results

Don't forget the Meta-Cognitive potential of the rubric

1. Internalize the writing process
2. Apply experiential learning
3. Incorporate prior learning
4. Situate the learning—place in a context

The following rubric is one that can be used for expository writing; specifically, for college-level courses at both the undergraduate and graduate levels. It can be used as a point of departure. By adding additional criteria, which tie directly to a specific writing occasion, it's possible to use the rubric at every step of the writing process, as detailed above.

	1: Poor	2: Fair	3: Adequate	4: Excellent	Score
Purpose Statement	Thesis or statement of purpose garbled or missing	Unclear purpose or thesis	Thesis / purpose statement is clear and coherent	Thesis statement is insightful and engaging	15
Audience Alignment	No recognition or acknowledgment of the audience's values, etc.	Inconsistent sense of audience; Uses language inappropriate to target audience	Conveys an accurate sense of audience with appropriate use of disciplinary language	Strong sense of audience demonstrated through form and language	10
Organization and development	Lack of clear progression of ideas or arrangement of background, evidence, or details	Unclear sequencing or rationale for the method of arrangement; weak connection to primary thesis in the body paragraphs	Ideas are connected clearly and they connect clearly to the primary thesis	Effective connections to the primary thesis, and a sequence that supports the logical arrangement and argumentation structure of the paper	20
Support for ideas	Incorrect, irrelevant, inaccurate, or biased evidence	Includes some, but not adequate support for arguments	The thesis and the evidence for the primary thesis are supported with clear, legitimate, and credible evidence, correctly cited	Supports the main idea and provides good support for points with credible, well-researched evidence and cites sources clearly	20

	1: Poor	2: Fair	3: Adequate	4: Excellent	Score
Understanding of Topic	Demonstrates little or no understanding of the topic or focuses on a topic that is not a part of the primary thesis	Demonstrates some understanding of topic; Does not make connections among ideas	Moves beyond surface understanding; Demonstrates facility with topical and disciplinary	Exhibits a deep understanding of the topic, background and interconnections; provides insight and new perspectives	20
Use of Grammar	Numerous errors in grammar, syntax, sentence structure or spelling	Occasional syntax, grammar, and spelling errors	Grammar, syntax, sentence structure and spelling are correct throughout document	Fluid, correct, and advanced use of language, with and extensive range of diction and syntactic variety	15
				Total Points / Percentage:	100

Plagiarism: Risky Swimming
Don't go near the Plagiarism Fish. Just one bite can be lethal!

Copying and pasting from the Internet.
It's a matter of degree and of attribution. Obviously, if you copy and paste an entire article from the Internet, even if you cite the source, it is considered academic dishonesty.

Some people copy and paste block quotes and they cite the sources correctly. However, their paper ends up looking like a patchwork quilt of quoted material that is essentially stitched together with thin transition sentences. This is not acceptable.

Your work should be your own, and you should not cite more than 15% from other sources.

"Blending" Unattributed Fragments

For some individuals, writing a paper is not writing at all. It is simply the assembly of a huge collage of fragments, paragraphs, sections, and bibliographies / literature reviews from material found in paper and digital sources. Usually, it is quite easy to detect this sort of plagiarism because the writing style is very disjointed.

If there is an authorial voice at all, it is that of a person with a sever personality disorder—multiple personalities, perhaps? In other words, consistency is lacking. The "blending" technique is usually evidence that the student feels insecure about his or her own ideas. It is not that the student is averse to working and conducting research; he or she is simply not confident about what to say or where.

Confidence can be built by developing clear thesis statements and defining specifically the goal of the paper. Further, it's important to let one have the free flow of ideas. A flowchart can often help one get started.

The instructor can also help by decriminalizing the expression of outre or unusual ideas, and becoming overly picayune and castigating students for grammar or typographical errors in the early drafts.

Turning in Work You Wrote for Another Class

You may not realize that turning in work you've done for another class is considered academic misconduct. Why?

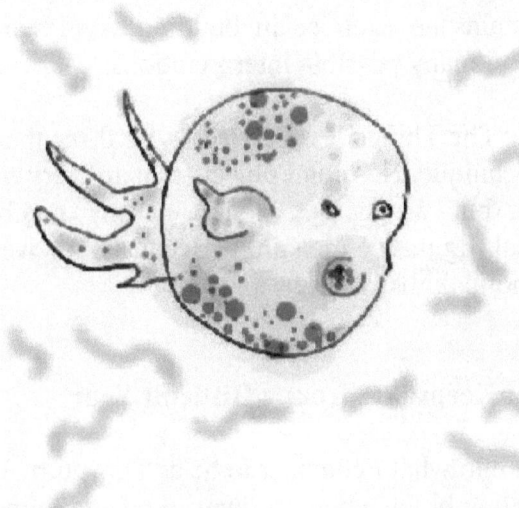

Worksheet: Vivid Writing

Building Figurative Meaning with Multiple Potential Interpretive Possibilities
Exercise—using figurative language / speaking images

One of the best ways to communicate an experience is to shape it around animal behavior, experiences with animals (ideally in the wild; animals in captivity and domesticated animals such as cats and dogs do not communicate the same message. The wild animals' behavior seems raw and honest).

Here is an exercise in generating ideas that can be fleshed out into metaphors you can relate to experiences in your life.

It also contains an exercise in building vivid sentences that lend themselves to many possible interpretations.

If you read "The Things We Carried," you'll see that the author used a similar technique. He found objects that are very material in and of themselves, but which also generated any number of affiliated metaphorical, figurative meanings. Because they were both concrete and metaphorical, they triggered

Example 1: Keepsakes from a Difficult Year

They all tie into what I consider to be a "Downturn Theme" and they relate to getting bitten, chewed, gnawed on and living to tell the tale.

My main keepsake is a taxidermied rattlesnake with a sample of Rattlesnake Limestone from a quarry near Austin, Texas, and I consider it perfect for representing how we have all been snakebit by the oil price collapse of 2014-2016, which is still ongoing at this writing. The rattlesnake is taxidermied so that its mouth is open to the point you can see deep into its white throat. Its fangs extend out and it doesn't take much at all to imagine venom dripping from them. I wonder how the guy who did the taxidermy avoided injecting himself with snake venom. I don't think I'd be able to!

Here is a list of animal-related items that represent to me the difficulties of the past year and a half:

- Snakebite Kit
- Fossil shark teeth (we got so tough that the shark got the worst of it when it tried to take a bite out of us)
- Photo of grizzly bear climbing on a pumping unit
- Photo of bear eating its young (as emblematic of what life was like in corporate America this year) http://www.earthweek.com/2009/ew091211/ew091211a.jpg

Example 2: Birds in Flight: Highs & Unexpected Lows

Things are going well! Turnaround, taking off, soaring high, reaching new heights—flying so high my feathers fall off (Icarus danger) or flying well (until I hit the jet engine!)

In this case, instead of developing a full paragraph or a paper around a concept, I'm going to try to use the concept to create a single sentence that contains a simile or a metaphor.

SENTENCES

Eagle soaring above a mountain
My sentence: I was like an eagle waking up to the cold winter air flowing under the downy-soft under-feathers of my wings.

Baby bird toppling out of the nest
My sentence: I was like that foolish little robin you see in early May – all beak, leathery, featherless skin and no common sense – who thinks the nest is just too tight for him and all his pushy little brothers and sisters.

Pelican diving for a fish – big splash! & then a big beak-full of fish
My sentences. I was a lucky treasure hunter – just like that big

pelican I used to watch outside my Pacific Ocean beach house at Lo de Marcos. Each time he plunged into the water, he came up with a beak full of plump, glistening *dorado*.

Canada goose flying high (and then right into a jet engine!)
My sentence: I was that cock-sure Canada Goose who could outrun the Boeing 737, until I realized that my race involved flapping my wings as hard as I could to escape the powerful currents of air pulling me right into the jet engines.

Bright parrot flying low in the rain forest
My sentence: He drove his car fast and recklessly – like a bright, half-insane parrot who flashed through the rainforest and mocked all the other birds with his piercing whistle.

Pigeon perched on the edge of a building about to take off
My sentence: I felt a certain restless and annoyed anticipation, like the pigeon who lived on the ledge next to my balcony, who would sit and wait until just the right half-eaten hamburger bun or donut landed next to the dumpster behind the QuikTrip next door.

One-Stop Shopping for Expository Essays
Descriptions of essay types and their characteristics

DESCRIPTION
https://owl.english.purdue.edu/owl/resource/685/03/

A description essay can be one of the most satisfying to write because you have the opportunity to spend time reflecting on the concrete details of a specific time, place, or event that you care about. For example, you might describe the naughty antics of your dog or cat (or iguana!)—and the action of describing become an affirmation of life itself, and most particularly, of a beautiful life as you know it. Now, even as I say "beautiful" I recognize that it's totally acceptable to plumb the depths of a zombie apocalypse while you're at it :)

Elements to include:

- "in medias res" opening (an illustrative scene)
- primary thesis (what is this about?)
- background / contexts
- use of sensory perceptions (visual, auditory, olfactory, gustatory (taste), tactile, etc.)
- specific details that trigger specific images in reader's mind ("drinking a Diet Mountain Dew straight out of the can", for example, instead of "drinking a soft drink")
- why does this matter?
- body paragraphs have a topic sentence that ties to primary thesis
- body paragraphs transition from idea to idea / scene to scene
- conclusion advances the main idea

NARRATIVE
https://owl.english.purdue.edu/owl/resource/685/04/

A narration essay is one in which you're telling a story. Question: do you have to tell the truth with your narration? Well. It depends. You can write a heart-warming account of your childhood, or you can totally invent a story about something fantastical and unlikely to ever transpire. The choice is yours. The key is to tell your story in a way that captivates your audience and keeps them hanging on every word. What makes people keep listening? It's often all about authenticity. Tell your story. Reveal things about yourself. Let yourself be raw and exposed. Show your humanity. Your audience will reach out and meet you more than halfway.

Elements to include:

- engaging "hook" in the opening paragraph "in medias res" opening (an illustrative scene)
- primary thesis (what is this story or narrative about)
- why does it matter?
- a bit of background
- develop the characters and the situation—make them unforgettable
- incorporate "flash memory" scenes that build the story
- body paragraphs have a topic sentence that ties to primary thesis
- body paragraphs transition from idea to idea / scene to scene
- conclusion either gives closure or leaves the reader wanting more

EVALUATION
http://www.aims.edu/student/online-writing-lab/assignments/evaluation

Ahh—this sounds a lot like Consumer Reports holding forth on the latest gas barbecue grills, doesn't it? But, not so fast! Evaluation is much, much more. It's all about connecting values and "wish list" with what actually exists in the phenomenal world. In other words, what do you think about the things you're seeing, doing, buying, and experiencing? That's evaluation. So, the key in writing about it is putting forth, first and foremost, what matters. What are the "must have" elements? And, then after that, what are the elements that make it good, bad, or sort of forgettable? When you're selecting something to evaluate, please be sure to find something you care about. Otherwise, the evaluation is likely to be tepid at best, and just flat forgettable at worst.

Elements to include:

- State what it is that you're evaluating
- Explain why it is that you need to evaluate it
- What matters about this thing? What are the "must-have" elements?
- Does this person, place, or thing measure up?
- Why or why not? How?
- Your evidence: must be convincing
- Thinking it through—are there ethical considerations? What are they?
- Wrapping it up—final thoughts and conclusions.

CAUSE AND EFFECT

http://ngl.cengage.com/assets/downloads/greatwi_pro0000000335/gw5_unit6.pdf

This happened, and that triggered this, that, and the other. Oh, yes—we understand the causal chain, and if we don't really know, we invent it. Causality is one of the most psychologically satisfying discursive forms known to man. And, why? Well, it's all about wanting to think we understand this world as we know it. And, it's also all about thinking we can do something about it. So, if eating raw puffer fish sushi will kill you—if a person dies after eating sushi, and we see it had puffer fish in it, then, we feel sort of comforted by the fact that we can manage our "life risk" which to say that if we love sushi, we can continue to eat it, but without including raw puffer fish. I say that assuming the person who is reading this (you, in fact), wants to keep on living.

Elements to include:

- The mystery, condition, or scientific phenomenon you're trying to untangle by exploring causal relationships
- Why does this matter?
- Step-by-step process
- The key assumptions
- What's wrong with this picture? Doubt and wondering... what are some of the possible problems?
- Cautionary tales? What are some of the things to keep in mind?

DEFINITION
http://www.wikihow.com/Write-a-Definition-Essay

Once upon a time, I wanted to nail down reality as an absolute. It was something that made me feel there was something to cling to—even my life itself proved itself to be all about mirage, illusion, mental invention, and raw courage. After struggling, I came to the conclusion that the "definition" is an act of will—it is a personal mission to assert a personal vision (in general) and a set of conditions (in particular) for the things that really matter to me.

Elements to include:

- The concept, thing, place, person, or phenomenon I plan to explore
- A bit of background—what's the context?
- Breaking it down: listing the aspects that contribute to an understanding of what this is
- Why should I care? Let's step back a bit and see what we're all about
- Raw thoughts and impressions: it's the knee-jerk responses that keep you engaged, right?
- A conclusion and summing up…and the next step…

ARGUMENTATION
https://owl.english.purdue.edu/owl/resource/724/1/

Alternatively called "taking a position," this is a assignment. You're working with pure persuasion, and your goal is to convince your reader of the legitimacy of your point of view. How you do that can be accomplished in many different ways. If you like the Ancient Greeks' approach, you'll focus on pathos (emotion), logos (logic), and ethos (tone and overall impression you make). Instead of looking at how to persuade someone, sometimes it's useful to think about how you would put together an utterly unconvincing piece of persuasive writing. Going about it that way can be fun—think about the big credibility destroyers out there.

Here are just a few: bias, incorrect facts, outright lies, personal attacks, emotional rants and diatribes, complete disregard for the audience's views and values, and random, Jackson Pollack-esque paint-splatter type of organization. It might even be fun to write something that fails miserably as a persuasive document. I hesitate to do so, though. What if it sticks and it's all I can do? I feel the same kind of hesitation I feel when I think about imitating a thick Southern accent. What if my mouth and voice "stick" and it's all I can do from now on? Scary! But, all rambling and ruminating aside, I think that the more we experiment with the argumentation essay and its form, the more we understand what's at the heart of persuasion.

Elements to include:

- The rhetorical situation—what do you want you reader to do after reading your paper? What do you want them to think, do, act, or express?
- Background and contexts—and mini-lit review if necessary
- Main idea / primary thesis
- Support for your idea—evidence paragraphs
- Body paragraphs—each topic sentence ties to the primary thesis
- The other side—accommodating other viewpoints

- Statistics, examples, case studies, testimonials—let's show how we can support everything we need to support
- Conclusion ... with thoughts, even if there are issues (pique curiosity—make your reader want to follow whatever you write)

Writing is about confidence ...

Writing for Business
with a Tourism / Hospitality Focus

Overview

Welcome to a series of short courses that will give you the tools you need to produce clear, high-impact writing that will help you attract clients, gain positive reviews online, and keep your on-site staff communicating and working together well.

Each module consists of writing for a specific occasion or purpose. You'll briefly analyze the each writing occasion or purpose, and you'll consider rhetorical situation, the goals, the audience. Then, you'll apply your knowledge using very easy-to-use guides and templates, which also include a checklist to follow as you revise your work, either by yourself, or with a team member.

The modules can be taken separately as individual mini-courses, or they can be bundled together and used within the framework of a larger course.

Each template involves the stages:

- Prewriting, brainstorming, outlining
- Writing a draft
- Revision / polishing

Process Writing: The Instruction Sheet

Introduction: Write a brief overview of the overall process, and include the main identifying factors that make it unique

Desired outcome and reasons for the process: Briefly explain the desired outcome or endpoint, and the reason for the process.

Contexts: Explain briefly where and how this takes place.

Ideal conditions: What are the ideal conditions? When can the process NOT be done?

Required Materials or Equipment: Prepare a list of the necessary equipment, along with any safety or size precautions

Step by step instructions: Either create a step by step procedure, or a checklist of things to do. Include criteria for quality.

Safety, security, and other considerations: Make a list of the issues of safety and security that need to be considered

Process Writing: The Instruction Sheet (Example)

The Fastidious Flamingo Restaurant
Procedures for closing the restaurant at night

Introduction: Write a brief overview of the overall process, and include the main identifying factors that make it unique

The Fastidious Flamingo Restaurant closes each night at 10 p.m. The purpose of this list of procedures is to assure consistency in closing each night

Desired outcome and reasons for the process: Briefly explain the desired outcome or endpoint, and the reason for the process.

The desired outcome is freedom from worry that the employees will either do too little or too much. The hope is that the procedure sheet will also eliminate communication problems and assure uniformity.

Contexts: Explain briefly where and how this takes place.

The procedure sheet will be used in the Fastidious Flamingo Restaurant for the employees. It will be used each night the restaurant is open.

Ideal conditions: What are the ideal conditions? When can the process NOT be done?

The process should start at around 8 pm, and be finished by 10 pm. Some of the tasks can be done while the restaurant is open, but it is important not to frustrate customers or interfere with their dining experience.

Required Materials or Equipment: Prepare a list of the necessary equipment, along with any safety considerations

Cleaning equipment, uniforms, also, consideration for wet floors and potentially toxic chemicals (detergent, bug spray, window cleaning chemicals)

Step by step instructions: Either create a step-by-step procedure, or a checklist of things to do. Include criteria for quality.

Step 1: Description   Time required:
Step 2: Description   Time required:
Step 3: Description   Time required.
Etc.

Safety, security, and other considerations: Make a list of the issues of safety and security that need to be considered

Safety considerations:
Security considerations:
Hygiene considerations:

PROPOSAL
Flowchart

Step 1: Start with a Need

Identify the need for the product, service, or information that you'd like to develop or provide.

_____
_____
_____
_____

Step 2: Identify the People or Organizations Involved

_____
_____
_____
_____

Step 3: Specify the Outcome

_____
_____
_____
_____

Step 4: Briefly Summarize How You Will Get to the Outcome

_____
_____
_____
_____

Step 5: Make a List of Key Action Steps or Activities

_____
_____
_____

Step 6: Desired Outcome for Each Activity—Initial Budget or Financial Outcome

_____
_____
_____
_____

Step 7: Expansions or Iterations? Briefly List Potential for the Future

_____
_____
_____
_____

Example of Developing a Proposal
Humanely Controlling Feral Hog Populations

Step 1: Start with a Need
Identify the need for the product, service, or information that you'd like to develop or provide.

Feral hogs cause tremendous damage to farms, ranches, park areas, and other spaces. They reproduce rapidly, and they destroy crops, pastures, roads, and they upset the ecosystem. Hunting is not always effective. The BoarBuster is a trap that can catch up to 50 hogs at a time, and it's operated remotely. It could be a good solution. Now, to optimize the use of the Boarbuster, it is necessary to know where the hog herds (sounders) are moving, roaming, foraging. To do that, drone surveys are recommended.

Step 2: Identify the People or Organizations Involved

- Landholder stakeholders (ranchers, municipalities, developers)
- Study developers (surveyors, computer experts, feral hog experts)
- Drone team (pilot, data processor)
- Solution provider (BoarBuster)
- Commercialization possibilities (mobile meat processing to create dogfood, etc.)

Step 3: Specify the Outcome

Drone pilots and surveyors will team up to provide services to landholder stakeholders who have a feral hog problem. They will then conduct drone surveys to identify the ideal placement of the BoarBusters to optimize the entrapment of sounders, and to be located near infrastructure (roads, electricity if needed).

Step 4: Briefly Summarize How You Will Get to the Outcome

We will conduct at least two drone surveys and then plan the implementation of the Boarbuster. At the same time, mobile meat processing possibilities will explored, and outlets for the processed meat (Dogfood? Human quality?) will be explored. If there are other aftermarket possibilities, they will also be explored.

Step 5: Make a List of Key Action Steps or Activities

- Identify locations with boar problems
- Contact ranchers / owners
- Assemble teams (drone pilots, GIS experts, data processing individuals)
- Contact BoarBuster and obtain information, feasibility, etc.
- Contact mobile meat processing
- Explore the possibility of combining tourism or education with the concept (field camp experience to learn how to do the studies? Day trip for tourists?)

Step 6: Desired Outcome for Each Activity—Initial Budget or Financial Outcome

- Eliminate damage to the crops or environment
- Provide valuable geographical information
- Develop new information gathering teams (new projects)
- Employment for the drone surveys
- Sales of Boarbusters
- Sales of mobile meat packing
- Sales of new dogfood or meat
- Tourism?
- Training seminars / education

Step 7: Expansions or Iterations? Briefly List Potential for the Future

The future is almost unlimited. If the proof of concept works, the surveys can be applied to wherever there are problem areas. Drone surveys are the first key integral step. Then, once more than one location is involved, careful project management will be required. Also, publicity and information dissemination of successful results will be a "must," along with lessons learned.

Learning what works

WE LEARN FROM EACH OTHER
AND, WE SHAPE OUR ARGUMENT BASED ON WHO
WE THINK OUR AUDIENCE WILL BE ...

Letter:

Dear BoarBuster:

I'm very interested in developing a project to conduct drone surveys over the most heavily feral hog-affected ranges and fields in South Texas (and other places).

I'd like to identify where the hog herds (sounders) travel, and then look at infrastructure to see where the road intersect with sounder roaming / foraging.

Then, I'd like to propose using the BoarBuster to solve the feral hog problem, with an idea of moving the BoarBuster from place to place in the ranch, park, pasture, woodlands, development, floodplain, etc.

The locations can be sited based on periodic drone surveys to keep up with the hogs.

I plan to develop a project during our upcoming workshop, and I hope to form several teams for different parts of Texas, Oklahoma, and perhaps other locations:

http://www.aapg.org/career/training/in-person/workshops/details/Articleid/33308/new-opportunities-with-drones-new-needs-faa-rule-changes-new-technologies

In anticipation of the event, I'd like to talk to you— ☺

I see this as a humane and cost-effective solution to a very serious problem. I look forward to being in touch. Please feel free to call my cell:

Using Flowcharts to Respond to Writing Assignments: Three Examples

Paper 1: People Under Stress

Assignment:
Write a brief paper (500–750 words) on stress impact on individuals, the family, the workplace, the community, and in society at large. The unit examines the sources of stress (war, terrorist attacks, domestic violence, bullying, economic uncertainty) and examines the methods currently used to detect, assess, and therapeutically deal with post-traumatic stress disorder (PTSD).

Flowchart / Guideline
You may use this flowchart to help you get started with your paper. You may follow it carefully, or you may use it as a starting point—a point of departure.

Alternatively, you can respond to the guiding questions or the points in the learning outcomes and objectives as detailed in the unit.

The choice is yours. Please use at least two outside resources. Cite them using APA.

Please keep in mind that flowcharts can be quite helpful in overcoming writer's block—even more helpful than an outline.

1 — Identify a situation in which war stress, post-traumatic stress syndrome, or general stress is having a negative impact on a situation.
 — describe the situation
 — describe the stress
 — how do you know that stress is having a negative impact? What evidence is there?

2 — Who are the impacted individuals? Who are they? How are they affected?

- Primary impact: describe the immediate situation and the context
- Secondary impact: describe the individuals who are impacted by the stress of those suffering from primary impact, explain how they are affected
- Tertiary impact: describe the general impact that primary & secondary impact has on the community, the workplace, total strangers

3 — Return to the situation. Analyze it in terms of changeable and non-changeable elements.
 — What can be changed?
 — What cannot be changed? How do you know?

4 — Focus on the changeable. Develop a series of action steps to be followed.
 — What will they be?
 — When are they to be implemented?
 — What is a general timeline? What are the major milestones? What are the steps that need to be taken under the category?

5 — Who are the primary people that need to be influenced in order to make the action steps and the general plan doable?
 — Who do you have to lead?
 — How do you lead? Leadership by example? Leadership by persuasion? Vision? Mission?

6 — Short-term goals.
  How did you select them?
  Are they realistic?
  How will you know if they have been achieved?

7 — Long-term goals.
  How did you select them?
  Are they realistic?
  How will you know if they have been achieved?

8 — Summary and overview.

Paper 2: Changing Perceptions, Changing Realities: Gender and Ethnicity

Assignment:
Write a brief paper (500–750 words) on the changing face of the American workplace and communities, and looks at the current state of affairs with respect to gender equity, race relations, ethnic or group stereotyping, affirmative action, and other issues in terms of equitable access to economic and educational opportunity

Flowchart / Guide
You may use this flowchart to help you get started with your paper. You may follow it carefully, or you may use it as a starting point—a point of departure. Please use at least two outside resources. Cite them using APA.

Write about what interests you and is relevant to your life. The choice is yours.

1 — Identify a culture clash in your organization. What are the groups and who are the members?
   — Describe the prevailing "cultures"
   — How is it apparent that there are conflicting cultures at play in this situation?
   — Delineate their defining values.
   — Point out areas of conflict. Describe an example and its possible consequences.

2 — Perception issues. How does one group perceive the other?
   — Problem points.
   — General issues.
   — Specific examples.
   — Are people manipulating others in order to profit from the culture clash? Why? How? When does it happen?

3 — Costs of Escalation. What are they? How and when does escalation happen? Provide examples of escalated ethnic, cultural, gender, or class / interest group clash.

4 — Perception Correction. How would you go about correcting perceptions and misconceptions? How would you de-escalate a situation? When and where are power issues a factor? How do people perceive their situation vis-à-vis power structures, the distribution of resources, economic access, a voice in community affairs, etc.?

5 — Insights gained from this analysis. List them. Comment on what it means to you, and your ability to work for positive change in your community, organization, or group.

Cabbages & Carrots

Finding similarities & differences

Paper 3: Team-Building Under Duress

Assignment:
Write a brief paper (500–750 words) on how to build effective teams in difficult times typified by a shortage of resources, funding, personnel, and/or time.

Flowchart / Guide
You may use this flowchart to help you get started with your journal. You may follow it carefully, or you may use it as a starting point—a point of departure. The choice is yours. Please use at least two outside resources. Cite them using APA style.

Please keep in mind that flowcharts can be quite helpful in overcoming writer's block—even more helpful than an outline. They can help you develop an effective outline, and they facilitate brainstorming, invention, and creative problem-solving processes.

1. Identifying the difficulties
    a. Resources. What are the resource difficulties? Are there shortages? List the items, then prioritize them by their impact on the overall mission.
    b. Funding. Identify funding difficulties. What is the impact on the mission. What are explanations for the funding difficulties. Propose solutions.
    c. Personnel. Identify problems in personnel (shortage, etc.). What is causing the personnel difficulties? Do the difficulties have to do with skills? Are the new personnel / team members new? Prioritize the difficulties, and make a "wish list" of a perfect solution in terms of personnel.
    d. Time. Describe the time difficulties. Not enough time? Why? What are the impacts of not having enough time?

2. Mission-critical needs.
    a. Which are the needs that, if not met, will result in harm to people?
    b. List the top three needs, in order of importance.

3. External factors.
   What are the major external factors (exogenous influences) that will impact the timely availability of resources, funding, and personnel?

4. Rapid rate of change. Quickly evolving scenarios, needs, problems. Where is the pace of change the most rapid?

5. Role reversal. Thinking from the other side.
   Is there a person in this situation who is placed in terrible difficulties? Which person would that be? How does the situation impact him or her, and what are the resulting difficulties on the rest of the team?

6. Making asymmetry work for you.
   Asymmetry: where there are huge imbalances (an oversupply of what you don't need, a shortage of things you do need). How can you use the imbalances in a positive way, which would result in a resolution of the difficulties?

7. Forecasting and projecting problem / difficulty scenarios, and rating the probabilities.
   List three different possible scenarios that involve difficulties of shortages of resources, funding, personnel, and / or time. Please state the likelihood of their occurring.

8. Forecasting and projecting solution scenarios, rating the probabilities.
   Propose a brief one or two-sentence solution for each of the three scenarios. Rate or state the likelihood of that outcome.

Writing to Explore an Ethical Dilemma: A Mini-Essay

Option 1: An Ethical Dilemma I've Observed

Please write a 2–3 page paper that has to do with a business ethics issue or topic in the text and connects to an experience you've had or observed. Examples could be the following:

1. Fried Rat: A restaurant buys frozen meat, thinking it's chicken pieces, but it turns out it's frozen rat from China. People love the taste of it, and it's cheap. You're thinking about buying the restaurant and you need it to make a profit. What do you do?

2. Hype Machine. The company that has a new medical device (an organ revitalizer) that could transform the medical industry as we know it. Now it's time to go to Wall Street and have an initial public offering. You're the CEO and you have a huge stock position. If you can get the price up, you'll be worth hundreds of millions. More importantly, you'll have capital to invest in the development and roll-out. But, can the "organ revitalizer" live up to the hype? What do you do?

3. DIY Cirque du Soleil. You've been to Las Vegas and have seen Cirque du Soleil. You have the idea that it would be great to start a Do It Yourself circus, where everyone has a chance try out everything. But, there are some definite ethical issues. What might they be? What can you do? How can you make it a viable business and successful as well.

4. My Own Most Dangerous Catch: Noodling for Catfish: You're putting together a fund-raising activity and would like to have a fishing contest. You live in a part of the country where there are quite a few catfish, but not much else. So, you've decided to make it a Noodling for Catfish contest. True enough, noodling can be dangerous. But, you think you've got it covered. What exactly are the risks of noodling? What will you do? Go ahead? Not go ahead?

5. Your own scenario. Here is a place to build your own ethical dilemma scenario and explore possibilities.

Option 2: An Ethical Dilemma I've Read About

Write a 2–3 page paper that analyzes a case study in your text or one that you have found. Please analyze it by responding to the following questions. Please use APA style. Your paper should be around 750 words in length.

- What is the underlying ethical issue?
- Who would be harmed? Who would benefit?
- Describe the ethical principle that applies to this situation.
- Describe a similar situation in your own experience or in a hypothetical situation that you could potential experience.
- Discuss what should be done. What are the consequences of not doing anything? What are the benefits of taking ethical action?

CASES FROM THE CRUZ-CRUZ (FREE) TEXT
https://ia800403.us.archive.org/11/items/ost-business-col10491/col10491.pdf
CASE 1: Mountain Terrorist Exercise (chapter 1)
CASE 2: Three frameworks for ethical decision-making (chapter 2)
CASE 3: Responsibility and Incident at Morales (chapter 3)
CASE 4: Pirate code for engineering ethics (chapter 4)
CASE 5: Toysmart (chapter 5)

Current Problem / Analysis Paper

Your paper may not have to be too long (5 or 6 pages), so you do not have to go into great detail. The main thing is to understand how to structure your paper, avoid repetition, and support your arguments. You should also know where to put valid references (using APA) style and to incorporate your own ideas and original analysis and thought.

Structure

Section 1: Main Idea / Primary thesis

Section 2: Background and Contexts: "The Big WHY"

Section 3: Evidence and Support: A Closer Look

Section 4: Responses, Controversies and Competing Ideas

Section 5: Contemplative Discussion

Section 6: Recommendations

Section 7: Conclusion

Example: Combatting Childhood Obesity

Section 1: Main Idea / Primary thesis
In this section, be sure to include the main idea in a very clear, succinct manner. The primary thesis should be one sentence either at the end or the beginning of the introduction. The thesis statement should give an indication of the overall structure of the paper and the aspects of the problem or topic that will be addressed.

Example: In the U.S., childhood obesity has become a serious problem with health, sociological, and psychological consequences.

Section 2: Background and Contexts: "The Big WHY"

This section contains historical background and it both limits and defines the scope of the research problem or topic.

Example (this is a rough draft): From 1990–2016, childhood obesity in the U.S. increased, with numerous negative consequences. Morbidly obese children, who weigh more than 20% more than the recommended guidelines, are not able to take part in physical activity, and often suffer from diabetes, asthma, (etc). They may have developmental delays due to the lack of socialization, and can be the subjects of bullying and "body shaming" both in person and via cyber-bullying. The societal consequences are significant, as law and regulations are passed to avoid discrimination, schools must deal with the physical consequences of having obese students, as well as bullying, and other phenomena. Issues of the causal factors require attention as well, as researchers struggle to determine the true causes: poor diet, contaminated food supply, lack of exercise, technological changes, social behavioral changes, etc.

Section 3: Evidence and Support: A Closer Look

This section goes into more detail but does not repeat the sections above. It provides additional support and examples. It should include statistics and information on other people who have done work in the field.

- The timeframe examined
- What has happened during that time?
    - CDC statistics
    - Other government statistics
- Who has written or studied the problem?
    - Psychological consequences (key thinkers / articles)
    - Health problems (key researchers / articles)
    - Sociological consequences (key researchers / articles)
        - legislation
        - policies
        - advertising / trends / new concepts
            - (body shaming, for example)

Section 4: Responses, Controversies and Competing Ideas

This section discusses the responses to the main problem and discusses if they have been effectives.

- What is being done?
- Is it working? Why or why not? Who says?
- Controversial points—what are the other sides of the issue?
- Give some examples of competing / other ideas

Section 5: Contemplative Discussion

This section can contain an in-depth discussion of a specific example that illustrates the entire issue. For example, in the case of childhood obesity, it could trace the story of a child of a mother who works three jobs, and who cannot provide a well-balanced diet. The case study analysis can be a platform for analyzing different aspects of the problem and providing insight by looking through different theoretical lenses.

Section 6: Recommendations

This section provides a summary of recommended steps, which should correspond to the earlier categories. In the case of childhood obesity, they fit well within the following:

- health
- psychological
- sociological

Section 7: Conclusion

The conclusion is a summary of the findings as well as a brief discussion of the road ahead.

Example:
BLOOD-SOAKED FEATHERS: URBAN FARMING MEETS URBAN FLOOD CONTROL-CREATED HABITATS

The stench of death hung heavily in the humid July air.

"I've already taken care of one fox. Now I'm going to take care of the other," snarled the fat, unshaven man standing in front of me. Sweat trickled down his grizzled white chin. Vultures were already circling overhead.

My heart sank. Just two weeks ago, I took photos of the shy and still endangered red fox which nosed his way through the fence from the flood-control wetlands that bordered my dad's acre of urban oasis. The fox had a distinguishing white spot next to his tail. Who would possibly want to kill such a beautiful creature?

The man let out stream of cursing under his breath. He most definitely had extermination on his mind. He loved his chickens. But, so did the foxes.

How had it come to this?

Collision Course in an Urban Context

The hallmark of being a good neighbor is tolerance and a "live and let live" attitude. That hallmark is something I take to heart. But, sometimes it leads to problems.

It started several years ago when the city decided to dramatically widen and deepen the small tributary that ran between neighborhoods in order to control flooding. Coincidentally, the neighbor decided to turn his tennis court and back yard into a place where he raised chickens.

I was appalled. On the one side of my dad's yard, the gently sloping concrete banks of the creek that created a lovely shaded park and garden walk up the heart of the town, had been turned into impassible wetlands, terrible for walking, but which easily handled torrential rains and runoff.

On the other side of my dad's yard, I saw the transformation of an architectural showcase into something else. The tennis court was a part of a home and a very large lot that had been the showcase for the most distinguished architect in town whose company had won the contracts to for almost all the public buildings in town. The home was split level and had a "Falling Water" Frank Lloyd Wright feel with its windows, integrated pool, gardens, and tennis court.

Here I reveal my aspirational elitism. I would have loved to have purchased that home (or at least, a home like it, since I would not to live in a house where the mother of my childhood friend committed suicide), and to have made it a showcase, even using it to host parties and get-togethers for family, friends, and colleagues. Who knows. With a home like that, I might achieve great things.

At least, that's the way that one of the American Dream success narratives goes. It is not one that I'm very comfortable with.
But to continue with how things were, a classmate and childhood friend (we were in Bluebirds and Campfire Girls together) lived there.

All was good until the suicide of her mother. The family sold the house and moved.

The house and grounds were carefully tended by the next owners until they moved.

And then, the new neighbors moved in, and no one knew what to make of them. Turning the half acre into an urban farming operation was a huge shift and it seemed the neighborhood took a plunge into the abyss of yards filled with rusty cars, boat trailers, and piles of rebar, concrete blocks, and "escombros." What was next? A landfill? Salmonella and avian flu outbreaks?

I preferred to look the other way. I heartily disapproved of the way they introduced chickens, and all I could think of was salmonella.

Lifestyle and Habitat Evolutions in an Urban Setting

But, their conversion of a *House & Garden* showpiece to vegetables, chickens, and outbuildings coincided with a national trend. "Organic mini-farms" and sustainability seemed to take the country by storm, and I felt very uncomfortable openly judging what I felt to be not at all in the spirit of "free range" and "urban farming."

Further, there were other urban gardens sprinkled throughout Norman, and I tended to think they were a great idea. I liked the idea of the "Farmer's Market" (although I do not know where one exists in this town), and the idea of the only food source being large commercial farms.

Widely celebrated urban farming projects in New York City, Chicago, and Lima have provided a great deal of satisfaction for those who work with the plants, and some produce enough produce to feed hundreds of people, even though they are on small plots of land. Further, they can alleviate the issue of "food deserts" in very poor communities, and provide access to affordable fresh produce.

In fact, urban farming has gained popularity. The Food and Agricultural Organization of the United Nations reports that 800 million city dwellers worldwide are involved in urban farming (http://www.fao.org/urban-agriculture/en/).

But, there are a few problems with urban farming, especially when there is animal husbandry and when the gardens are not weeded, and attract mice, rats, snakes, and more.

In my father's neighborhood, and urban farming experiment would have a dramatic impact on the neighbors. With the exception of my father's land, and a few others, most of the homes were on tight little square lots.

Urban Farming's Unexpected Dark Side

The city-engineered flood control wetlands introduced a whole host of other health issues, but there seemed to be little one could do about it. Water moccasins, potentially rabid skunks, coyotes, and rats were among the less desirable new inhabitants of the new habitat.

Anything that took place in the neighborhood would most definitely affect the health and safety of a large number of people; in fact, the street they lived on was a major north-south access road for many of the town's most visited destinations (the University, a basketball stadium, baseball fields, and more).

The chickens (which I studiously avoided looking at; the sight of the abused tennis court felt like a racquet smacking my leg) ... multiplied.

The chickens (and their eggs) attracted mice, snakes, opossums, raccoons, coyotes, foxes, crows, and more, who were, after all, right on the edge of the urban farm.

I believe that the regular way to deal with such pests is to keep the area clean and to use chicken wire.

But, that was not to be.

Once, three years ago, after finding a 7-foot snake (clearly headed toward the eggs) and being visited by at least 3 different opossums, and seeing hawks circling overhead, it started to be fairly apparent that the wetland fauna were migrating toward the urban farm. The robins, mockingbirds, squirrels, rabbits, cardinals, finches, and raccoons had company.

Watching Too Many Episodes of "Forensic Files"?

And suddenly, they did not. One day, my dad commented that every single living thing had suddenly disappeared from his yard.
It was just at that time that the neighbor, a professor at the university, who spent hours each day nurturing her Oklahoma wild flower garden, collapsed with seizures which seemed to come from nowhere. She had never had any illnesses at all, and was an avid cyclist and folk dancer.

Silent summer. Silent fall.

Then slowly, slowly, after two unusually rainy years, the animals re-established themselves, and my dad's yard was alive again with birds frolicking in the bird baths, squirrels, rabbits, crows, and even the two adorable foxes—a mother and her kit—who spent time in the back extent of the yard, near the creek.

And then, again, all fell silent.

Coincidentally, a day after all fell silent, my dad had an attack of vertigo and complained that he could barely move. His frailty was frightening.

Then, it became clear that someone had been sprinkling poison in my dad's back yard. It was becoming airborne in the stiff southern breeze and blowing directly into the home with the windows always kept a few inches open for fresh air, and the patio door left open for fresh air.

And, for the first time, I realized that my desire to be tolerant, and my secret shame of being a snob, had endangered the neighborhood. The chicken excrement washed directly into the creek, which was a major watershed, going directly into one of the most important rivers in this part of the state.

The chickens were victims, too. They looked miserable in their habitat, and undoubtedly, they were not only in dirty, cramped quarters, where they could get sick, but they had to watch as their brothers and sisters were mutilated by foxes and coyotes. I felt very sorry for them.

If the man had become attached to his chickens, I could partially understand his desire to eliminate any possible threat.

Paranoia or Prudence? A Narrative Without Closure

But…poison???

Setting out poison would contaminate the watershed.

The poison could contaminate the topsoil, and if airborne, cause health problems for all who were in contact: neighbors, people working in construction, landscapers, visitors.

The man continued to shout and his face turned red. I looked at the 8 old vehicles he parked in the yard, and images of "Ranch Apocalypse," David Koresh, and Waco, Texas, came to mind. I felt a surge of uncertainty. He could be dangerous.

The hot breeze pushed the heavy smell of death and I felt a surge of nausea. The hallmark of a good neighbor is not tolerance. It is mutual respect.

The shadow of a vulture flitted across the lawn. I looked at the creek which had been expanded and re-engineered to provide better flood protection. One had to blame the city planners for part of the problem, because the wetlands they had created were the ideal habitat for opossums, red foxes, coyotes, squirrels, water moccasins, and more within the city limits.

Further, as an important tributary of the South Canadian River, all the weed killers, synthetic fertilizers, and other lawn care chemicals flowed directly into the watershed.

But, I never saw any sort of public awareness campaign to protect the watershed, or to instruct people how to interact with the wildlife and how to appreciate the diversity, rather than resorting to trapping and killing what interfered with your selfish human-centric plans. It gave rise to ethical issues. Which lives matter? Animal? Human? Both? None? And when confronted by the expedient decisions, there were hard realities to face.

Convenience or conscience?

Someone would have to decide.

The Research Process

It's about planning and breaking down the work into manageable steps.

Getting Started
- Define your research problem
- Make a list of key words that you can use in a keyword search
- Make a preliminary lists of relevant authors and researchers in this field

Step One: Keyword Searches

- Internet search: try search engines such as http://www.northernlight.com and http://www.google.com for searches for material on the web, but be very discerning as to the suitability of the material for your paper

- Journal search: determine the field of study you need to research. Is it in the Humanities? Earth Sciences? Life Sciences? Social Sciences? Search in the appropriate databases

- Monograph and book search: go to the library and conduct a keyword search, and also search based on the results found in your journal and Internet searches (authors, titles, journals)

Step Two: "The Concept"

Write down what you consider to be the major concept encapsulated in your research problem; that is, the key results or contributions that your research will yield.

Look through the material that you have found in your earlier searches and make a list of authors, new keywords, journals.

Search again, filling in the gaps so that you can find articles that clearly articulate aspects of the concept of your research problem, either in previous times or currently.

Step Three: Finding "Evidence"

What constitutes "evidence" that backs up your research problem? Make a list of the types of evidence—does it consist of statistics? Of passages from books? Of artworks? Of critical articles or critical analyses?

Make a list of the key individuals who have generated the types of evidence you need to find. These may be a) researchers; b) authors; c) writers of critical theory or criticism; d) scientists.

Return to journals, Internet, and library indices and find additional articles or works that you can use as evidence. Be sure to keep track of all the information you will need to create a proper citation.

Step Four: Chronicling the History and Development of Ideas Pertaining to Your Research Problem

Write down what you consider to be the primary research problem, and list the evolution of ideas pertaining to it.

Who were the first people to write about the problem, as it existed in its nascent form?

What was your research problem topic or theme called in earlier times? Did it have the same name? Who gave it that name? What were the socio-political implications?

Return to your sources and create a timeline that traces the evolution of ideas, research activities, theories, and propositions relating to your research problem.

Step Five: Researching "The Opposition"

Are there any articles or books that you have come across in which the author takes a position that is diametrically opposed to your own vis-à-vis your research problem?

Who and why do they have different ideas concerning the same research problem or topic?

What are their ideas?

Research these and list them.

Step Six: Putting It All Together

Review your paper and underline the passages that require support or substantiation. Find the appropriate reference and place it there.

Add a "Definitions" section. Define your terms from the articles you have found. Cite them properly.

Add a "Backgrounds" section and describe the history and evolution of ideas regarding your research problem. Be sure to include the dissenting views (the "opposition") to provide a balanced approach.

Review the correct style guide and make sure that you are following the proper citation style. If it is in the area of humanities, it will probably follow MLA or Chicago style; if the social sciences, APA. If science, consult the discipline and find out the appropriate approach and the rationale for it so that you understand precisely why the references are listed as they are. Be sure to differentiate between Internet sources, journals, newspapers, interviews, and monograph/books.

Research Paper Survival Guide & Flowchart

Getting Started
- What's your primary thesis & your research problem?
- Three major sections or thrusts of your research.
- One-sentence overview of your findings, or what you think makes this paper valuable.

Definition Section
- Define key terms needed to understand your paper.
- Cite references.

EXPANDED Key Research Problem
- In-depth look at your problem; go into more detail.
- Begin to organize your references, check the credibility of all sources.
- Background and Contexts
- Explain why your approach is unique
- Brief chronology of other work done; brief history of ideas & research in this specific area.
- Overview of key works in this area.

"Evidence" Section
Present your evidence. Remember that "evidence" can take different forms. It could consist of examples, case studies, articles, original research, supporting statistics. Explain why the evidence you use is valid

Expanded "Evidence"—Further Case Studies & Original Conclusions
In-depth analysis

Debate Points / Controversy / Insight
Is there anything about this topic that is controversial? Are there two sides of the issue? What are they? Who thinks so? Why? Cite sources.

Concluding Summary
Insights, analysis, recommendations

References
Refer to the style guide, and cite all sources, including journals, books, monographs, Internet-based sources. Double-check the credibility and/or reliability of the information—ask your advisor or your librarian.

Cite sources using the style appropriate to the topic.

Organization:

Grouping your thoughts and ideas in similar themes

Placing the most important in positions of prominence

Research Paper Getting Started Freewrite
Dog Whisperer Massive Fail

I just returned from visiting a friend in Guadalajara, and after I returned home, it occurred to me that there was something different about the dog. The last time I visited, there was a German Shepherd, a Rottweiller, a 9-month-old Rottweiler-Shepherd mix, five Rott-Shep puppies, and a small hyperactive (although sort of obese) rat terrier.

The puppies had been given to a friend with a place in the country near San Miguel Los Altos. I did not pay too much attention to the ones who were left—I just tried to stay away so they would not jump up on my white skirt.

Later, after I was home, I was thanking my friend for a nice stay, and I mentioned to him that I did not see little Zeus, the rat terrier. He said to me, "Oh. Didn't I tell you? You know what happened, right?"

I paused. "Uhhh. No…?"

He proceeded to tell me that he had to be away from the house for a little over a week, and although he had someone watching the dogs, something terrible had happened. Somehow, little Zeus, the rat terrier, turned up dead. Killed by another dog (or dogs).

!!!!

I was horrified. First, little Zeus was hyper and was always stealing food from the others—and, they about 3 times his size. But who would have ever suspected that he would be mauled—murdered!—by his buddies!!

So horrible. I felt very sad & it brought home to me that it's very important to protect your pets from each other. You never know when one will snap and harm the others.

I know it is a bit controversial—how to deal with disruptive dogs, etc. I do not advocate putting them down. But, I do think they have to have a safe environment.

Honestly, I wonder if my friend is a bit worried. I mean, if they've killed once, when will they do it again???

Questions:
This is a draft based on a free-write from a remembered event.
What are some of the deeper issues at work here?
How can the deeper issues be incorporated?
What would the main idea of the essay be, given the deeper issues?

Research Paper Overview

http://www.beyondutopia.net/writing-survival-guide/guide1/

Structuring your paper to guide the reader to your findings, encourage active dialogue, and to clearly present your original analysis.

Structure

I. Brief presentation of your primary thesis, your research problem, three major sections of your investigation, and the solution / findings / recommendations that you will be making.

Overview: In this section, you present a clear, brief, and eminently lucid summary of your problem and subsequent investigation. The description of your primary thesis should not be more than one sentence in length. In a subsequent sentence, you will describe three major aspects that you investigate in your paper. You should briefly state why this is important, and that you are taking a unique approach to the problem.

Keys to Success: Be brief, clear, and direct. You should engage the reader's the interest by indicating what makes your work worthwhile, unique, potentially useful. Keep in mind that you are laying down the foundation for rest of the paper, and creating a category that your reader can easily manage and archive. You are preparing a pathway for your reader and facilitating the process of making relevant connections, and the application of the reader's own experience to the points you are making. You are also creating an ethos or tone that is highly credible, which will place your reader in a frame of mind that is receptive and accepting of your "evidence" and "proofs."

Example: This paper examines the use of utopian narratives in Native American science fiction and explores how they function to a) propose new visions of a world which incorporate traditional Native views of the human's relation to nature, b) propose an alternate vision of science fiction, and one that does not primarily concern itself with a dialectic between the human and the machine, and c) envision communities of the future that incorporate Native-based systems of governments. Although there have been a number of studies of Native American writers, none have looked at this aspect of writing, nor have they examined the cultural beliefs, underlying assumptions about human nature and the proper role of government, or the ethics of technological innovation vis-a-vis a core sense of humanity. This investigation focuses primarily on the work of three Native American writers, and approximately 25 collections of their novels, essays, short stories and poems.

II. Definition of key terms and concepts. Cite references.

Overview: In this section, you will provide definitions and descriptions to terms that are central to the development of your paper. This is not the same as a glossary, but is more of a definition and discussion of how you use the term in your paper. For example, one could say "Holman's Handbook to Literature defines a 'utopian narrative' as 'xxx xxxx xxxx xxx' (Holman 762)" Only define the terms that the average reader is not likely to understand, or the terms that have a special application for your paper.

Keys to Success: Make a list of key terms and concepts that you are addressing. Look very closely at terms that may be in common parlance, but which have a special and specific meaning or application for your research paper. Be clear, and explain the specifics when necessary. Cite sources.

III. The research problem, further described. An in-depth look at your research problem, which describes what it is, with an illustrative scenario or example. This a synthesis and should be original work, therefore it may not be necessary to cite sources here. If there are controversial elements, mention them briefly.

Overview: This gives you a chance to re-address the topic you introduced in the first section and to go into more detail. You may be able to simply describe the issues and why there is a sense of urgency about the topic. If your topic is an exploration of a social issue, or a proposed method, you may wish to further describe your topic with an illustrative example or scenario which shows rather than tells the reader the central issue.

Keys to Success: Develop this section well so that your reader has a clear idea of the depth and complexity of the research problem, and an understanding of the major issues. Select your illustrative scenario very carefully so that it does not set up contradictions or conflicts with later sections of your paper. Without becoming sentimental, or generating bathos, this section can evoke an emotional response which can be helpful in persuading your reader of the importance of the study.

IV. History of research on this topic. Explain why your research is unique and needed. Give a brief chronology of research, and the history of ideas. Provenance, antecedents, etc. Cite sources.

Overview: This section is invaluable, not only to your reader but also to yourself because it compels you to research your topic very carefully and to trace any evolution of ideas that might have occurred. In addition, it makes your argument solid and gives it credibility. It demonstrates that you, as a researcher, are well aware of the work that has been done in the area.

Keys to Success: Keep the lines of investigation clear and focused. Do not list articles that digress or do not specifically refer to your primary thesis and the research problem. Try to find the source of some of the key ideas and trace the evolutionary unfolding and adoption of the ideas as they relate to your primary thesis.

V. "Evidence" section. Supporting statistics, examples, case studies, citations, supporting passages from key texts. Explain why the statistics you cite are valid. Present counter-arguments and opposing viewpoints. Cite carefully.

Overview: In this section, you present supporting findings from credible sources. These generally take the form of refereed journals, books by respected publishers, monographs, and online journals. In the case of online references, you will need to be very careful to assure yourself that the source is credible. If in doubt, ask your advisor or librarian.

This is where you present statistical support for your idea, and/or the results of any research, surveys, laboratory investigations, etc. Be sure to discuss methodology as well as addressing who conducted the research, when it was done, why or what primary objective was served, where it happened, what results were obtained. If research was conducted that refutes or calls into question this work, be sure to describe it as well.

Keys to Success: Make certain the statistics are directly relevant to your research problem, and clearly describe how they relate to the primary thesis and/or the sub-topics or aspects explored. Set the stage to be able to refer back to this supporting evidence when making points in later sections of the paper.

VI. Expanded "Evidence"—Further case studies or examples. Minimum of three: supporting your thesis statement, one that takes your thesis statement in a new direction or explores the subtopics, and one that makes one think of new aspects of your thesis and research problem. Use citations, and intersperse your thoughts and analysis throughout.

Overview: This is part of the research paper where your analytical abilities are put to the test. This is also where you have a chance to show the reader the key elements of your argument, and elements those elements with examples. It is necessary to be very careful in citing sources. Your mission here is to demonstrate that your ideas and insights are rock-solid, and if they dare doubt, you have the facts to back it up!

Keys to Success: Find good examples or case studies that clearly illustrate the points you want to make. Do not quote passages that are too long: make it short, pithy, and relevant. Be sure to discuss the quote, and do not place two block-quotes together, or one after another in concatenation. Your discussion should make connections between your primary thesis, the subtopics, and any new or interesting insights you have or discoveries that you have made. Be sure to cite your sources.

VII. Debate points or controversial aspects. Discuss the issues and present new ways of looking at the primary thesis, and its three or four primary sub-categories. This is your original work. Begin to undermine or question the underlying assumptions that may problematize your investigation, and your conclusion, approaches, solution.

Overview: This is the "fun" part of the paper. Here you have a chance to bring up all the controversial points, points of debate, and potential conflicts and/or contradictions. A good way to get started is to address any stereotypes or myths that might be associated with your topic, and which get in the way of a clear-headed, down-to-earth, and rational analysis of the facts. You may also wish to dig into the underlying assumptions in your work. These can be cultural assumptions, or underlying ideas about the nature of people, ideas about society and government, or ethical issues. In addition, you have a chance to explore the impact of current trends or ways of thinking and explore those. If there are troubling and potentially contradictory underlying issues that often come to the surface as you are thinking about your research problem, please be sure to address them here. If they occur to you, they will most certainly occur to at least some of your readers. By addressing them, you are making a concession to them, and demonstrating that you are in full command of the facts and the issues. This will help your credibility. In addition, you have a chance to explain why the approach you used is the most appropriate, and why you selected the case studies and/or examples that you did. You can also explore the implications that the subject you explored have on the future.

Keys to Success: Be direct, and don't be afraid to address controversy. Lay your cards on the table. Demonstrate why this topic is fascinating, and why your research problem is so intriguing that you would choose to devote a good segment of your valuable time and resources to it. If you're excited, your audience will be excited, too.

VIII. A concluding summary that is more than a conclusion. Insights, recommendations, probable issues vis-a-vis the future. This can include a vision of the future, an illustrative scenario.

Overview: In this section, you bring together your research, your analysis, and your insights, and you lead your reader to a brief contemplation of where they have been as they traveled through your paper. You have a chance to explain why this paper is relevant to future studies and investigations. If you are making a recommendation which would require the reader or someone to take action, then you can develop action steps, and even develop an illustrative scenario to help the reader envision your ideas.

Keys to Success: Do not be too reductive or narrow. Instead, reinforce the importance of the research. Be specific, and avoid being too universal or general.

IX. References. Please be sure to refer to the APA Style Guide or another commonly accepted style guide and clearly cite all sources: journals, books, reference materials, Internet-based information.

Revising Your Paper

Don't panic! You can get help from the most unexpected sources...

Structural Revisions
- Look at the basic structure of your paper. Are you missing key sections?
- Pay careful attention to your first section. Does it cover the material you have presented in the body of your paper and in the discussion?
- Confused? Refer back to the Writing Papers Survival Guide

Undeveloped Ideas Expansion
- Read each section carefully
- Where you find an unsubstantiated point, write in the margin "Need Evidence."
- Where you find an unclear chain of ideas, or a clear exposition of antecedents or the evolution of your research problem, write "Need History of Ideas Backup"
- Where you need to expand your explanation or definitions of terms, write, "Need Definitions or Clarification"
- Where you need to develop a connection, insight, or conclusion, write "Expand My Own Thoughts Here!!! Cool Stuff!! My ideas!!"
- Where you find yourself rather confused, write, "Clarify, Please!"

Repetition Elimination
- Read each section carefully
- Do you repeat phrases or words within a paragraph? Circle these in red.
- Do you repeat entire concepts or discussions from section to section? Circle the repeated or redundant passages in red.
- Do you use one example or source too much, and do you overlook others? Note this on the side in the margin.

Organizing and Repositioning Sections
- Do your paragraphs flow? Do they make sense logically? If not, indicate where they should be repositioned.

- Are your points presented in a consistent manner? Does your evolution of ideas flow in a chronological manner?
- Do you need information from one section in order to understand another? Be sure to put your foundations paragraphs before the ones that include conclusions or analyses dependent upon information in certain passages.

Grammar and Style
- Read carefully for a) verb-subject agreement; b) sentence fragments; c) run-on sentences (comma splices).
- Make certain your citations are correct.
- Read carefully to assure yourself that your style and tone are consistent throughout.
- Ask another person to read carefully and find copy-editing problems (spelling, typographical errors, inconsistencies) or tone / ethos problems.

Writing Literature Reviews

A literature review is a vital tool in being able to describe relevant research and findings on a topic that is of interest to you. A good literature review enables you to conduct research effectively, read articles critically and proactively, and to organize the knowledge. It also gives you the ability to rank and classify articles and their authors, and to determine whether or not their work is relevant and credible, and how it can provide insights and answers to your questions.

Two types of literature reviews:

Literature Review Essay:
This is an essay that describes the topic, the importance of the topic, and then provides a summary and overview of significant research in the topic, along with discussion of how, where, why and when the articles are meaningful, and what they contribute.

The discussions of the articles include the following:

>A sense of the unfolding / evolving nature of the topic
>An idea of who are the main researchers in the topic
>An overview of some of the research challenges in the areas
>Possible problems and challenges likely to be encountered

Pros of the Literature Review Essay:
>Gives you an opportunity to synthesize the essays
>It forces you to put things in order
>Makes you consider how thinking about the topic has evolved over time
>Forces you to uncover the underlying assumptions as you contemplate the history of the idea
>Helps you compare and contrast the essays, leading to qualitative determinations

Cons of the Literature Review Essay:
>You may jump to conclusions because you're synthesizing too soon

- You may not have enough information to compare effectively
- You may not be able to find enough material to construct an accurate evolutionary timeline
- Once you've come to conclusions, you may not maintain an open mind
- Your discussion / synthesis of the articles may not contain enough information from each article
- You may be tying yourself to a topic that is too narrow or that cannot be modified

Examples:
http://faculty.mwsu.edu/psychology/Laura.Spiller/Experimental/sample_apa_style_litreview.pdf
http://libguides.uwf.edu/ld.php?content_id=19806265

Literature Review Annotated Bibliography:
Articles or other sources are listed and a paragraph appears underneath the citation. The paragraph describes the article and includes the following information:

one-sentence nano-summary
how does it to the research topic?
what makes it useful?
what are the nuggets of information you'll use in a report?

Structure of the Annotated Bibliography Literature Review

- Title of your proposed paper
- One-sentence description of your topic / research problem (or research problem statement)
- List of your articles (using APA citation style)
- Groupings / clusters based on the category of article
    - Definition
    - Background / contexts / statistics
    - Case Studies
    - Controversies

Pros of the of the Annotated Bibliography form of a literature review:
    You can go in-depth with the articles
    You can explore different definitions
    It is easy to explore different categories of articles
        Definitions
        Philosophical or theoretical implications / foundations
        Case studies
        Studies
        History of the idea (or the problem)
    Easy to remind yourself of the value of each article
    Excellent for transferring to your essay in APA format
    Easy to update and expand
    Can use easily with databases

Cons of the Annotated Bibliography form of a literature review:
    It is not easy to synthesize the information from all of the sources
    It may be difficult to organize the information in order to see the evolution of the concept
    You do not have the opportunity to write an introduction and thus expand subtleties

You may tend to be tied to certain types of information (articles from databases, for example)

Examples:
https://library.ithaca.edu/sp/assets/users/_lchabot/lit_rev_eg.pdf

Literature Review: Useful Online Databases for Human Relations

EBSCO
Provides access to a multidisciplinary collection of over 50 databases covering the social sciences, humanities, and sciences. Select the databases most appropriate for your research topic and search them simultaneously. Some full text available.

DOAJ
https://doaj.org/
DOAJ is a community-curated online directory that indexes and provides access to high quality, open access, peer-reviewed journals.
9,176 Journals
6,365 searchable at Article level
130 Countries
2,256,073 Articles

Emerald Insight
Emerald is a global publisher linking research and practice to the benefit of society. Founded in 1967, Emerald today manages a range of digital products, a portfolio of nearly 300 journals, more than 2,500 books and over 450 teaching cases.

Project Muse
Project MUSE is a leading provider of digital humanities and social sciences content; since 1995, its electronic journal collections have supported a wide array of research needs at academic, public, special, and school libraries worldwide. MUSE books and journals, from leading university presses and scholarly societies, are fully integrated for search and discovery.
MUSE currently includes:

399,081 articles and 960,012 chapters by 257 publishers

ProQuest
ProQuest includes dissertations and theses (full-text, downloadable as PDFs), as well as articles from periodicals and peer-reviewed journals.

Government statistics
    FedStats: Gateway to statistics from more than 100 agencies.
        https://fedstats.sites.usa.gov/
    ChildStats: Child and Family Statistics.
        http://www.childstats.gov/

World Bank and United Nations free sources
    The World Bank Open Knowledge Repository:
        https://openknowledge.worldbank.org/
    UNData: United Nations Data
        http://data.un.org/Default.aspx

Databases with articles and full-text monographs:
    Business Source Premier
    EBSCO host
    JStor
    Project Muse
    Proquest
    PsycARTICLES
    Social Theory
    SocINDEX
    The SAGE Handbook of Mental Health and Illness
    Wall Street Journal Historical Newspaper
    Women and Social Movements in the United States

    DOAJ (Director of Open Access Journals): https://doaj.org/

Literature Review Topic Selection

The first step in developing your literature review is to select a topic that interests you, and which has interested writers and researchers so that there are credible, reliable articles that present many facets of the issue, and also different points of view.

Here are a few questions that will help guide you in your selection:

What are the top four or five topics that you'd like to research?

_____
_____
_____
_____
_____

What are the aspects of the topics that interest you most? Why could it be considered to be an important topic?

_____
_____
_____
_____
_____

Have there been any recent controversies or developments that have brought the topic to the attention of researchers, writers, or the general public?

_____
_____
_____
_____
_____

What are some of the underlying social, psychological, or economic issues embedded in the topics?

_____
_____
_____

Where are a few places where you've seen the topic addressed? (online news articles? Journals? Videos? Interviews with people you know?)

Literature Review: Planning Worksheet

As you prepare to launch your literature review, here are a few questions to answer. They will help you focus and organize your thoughts.

One-sentence summary of the main focus of your research:
_____
_____
_____
_____

General Subject Area:
_____
_____
_____
_____

My purpose for being interested in this is:
_____
_____
_____
_____

Best Search Terms for search engines or databases:
_____
_____
_____
_____

Best Search Sources
Web-based sites (government databases / search engines / open access journals)

_____
_____
_____
_____
_____

Databases (online library, etc.):
_____
_____
_____
_____

Literature Review: Single Annotated Bibliography

FLOWCHART 1
Flowchart for a SINGLE REFERENCE in the Annotated Bibliography

My topic:
_____

Article Citation: (APA Style)
_____
_____
_____
_____

Article Overview & Analysis—

a. One-sentence nano-summary.
_____
_____
_____
_____

b. Key quote that illustrates the major significance (quote should be followed by a parenthetical citation, with References to follow. Inside parentheses: Author followed by year).

The main area of significance of the article is...
_____
_____
_____
_____

c. Most important aspect of the article / study and why.

_____
_____
_____
_____

d. What this article means to me in the world at large and to the field.

_____
_____
_____
_____

Personal Opinions and Conclusions: These are my thoughts and ideas after reading the articles, doing more investigations on the topic, etc.

_____
_____
_____
_____

Recommendations, Insights, Ideas for Future Study:
Did I learn much from these articles & my subsequent research? What was it? What will I do next? What recommendations would I make to the researchers? My conclusions.

_____
_____
_____
_____

Another more recent article

_____
_____
_____

A unique, reliable resource I found on the web:

Example of the Annotated Bibliography for a Single Source

Now you can start putting the pieces together as you conduct your research. Please analyze the following example and use it as a guide to complete an analysis of the topic and some of the articles you have found.

EXAMPLE

My topic: Cyberbullying

Citation:
Froeschle, J., Mayorga, M., Castillo, Y., & Hargrave, T. (2008). Strategies to Prevent and Heal the Mental Anguish Caused by Cyberbullying. *Middle School Journal, 39*(4), 30–35. Retrieved from http://www.jstor.org/stable/23048097

Article Overview & Analysis—

a. **One-sentence nano-summary.** This article reports findings from a team of middle school counselors who seek solutions to technological victimization. The article provides a good definition and explanation of cyberbullying as well as 9 implementable strategies.

b. **Meaning and major significance (quote should be followed by a parenthetical citation, with Works Cited to follow. Inside parentheses: Author followed by year).**
The main area of significance of the article is in profiling the perpetrator and the victim, and then designing and implementing a collaborative program that involves school administrators, teachers, and parents. This article contains nine separate suggestions that can help deter and curtail cyberbullying in a middle school environment. "Cyberbullies consist of two types of individuals: social climbers and aggressive harassers." (Froeschle, et al, 2008)

c. Most important aspect of the article / study and why.
The application of theories that could provide immediate relief / solutions for a school.

d. What this article means to me in the world at large and to the field.
It's a good first step. The suggestions may not be appropriate for all schools, and they may need to do more to address the underlying issues in the school that could be perpetuating bullying.

Personal Opinions and Conclusions: These are my thoughts and ideas after reading the articles, doing more investigations on the topic, etc.

I'm not quite convinced that all the solutions are equally implementable. Also, I think that the article fails to address the ways in which organizations, groups, and social networks unconsciously reward bullying behavior.

Recommendations, Insights, Ideas for Future Study:
Did I learn much from these articles and my subsequent research? What was it? What will I do next? What recommendations would I make to the researchers? My conclusions.

I need to do more work. I am going to look at more articles—not just from refereed journals, but also from online magazines, etc.

Here is another example, from 8 years later. Clearly cyberbullying continues to be a problem. According to this article, cyberbullying potentially contributes to the No. 2 cause of teen death: suicide.

Plumber, Q. (2016) The Growing Scourge of Cyberbullying, Part 1. *TechNewsWorld.* August 10, 2016.
http://www.technewsworld.com/story/The-Growing-Scourge-of-Cyberbullying-Part-1-83789.html Accessed August 10, 2016

The Cyberbullying Research Center is an excellent resource for parents, educators, teens, law enforcement, counselors, and more.
http://www.cyberbullying.org

It contains articles, resources, definitions, and more, and it provides advice on such topics in cyberbullying as:

- sexting
- Snapchat safety
- Social media safety
- Revenge porn
- Extortion via cyberbullying
- Cyberbullying stories

Let your ideas grow:

Give them space

Intersperse them with the unexpected

Water

Watch

Enjoy!

LITERATURE REVIEW: Multi-Article/Reference Annotated Bibliographies

FLOWCHART 2

FLOWCHART for the full Annotated Bibliography (5 core sources that have full annotations)

Topic
_____
_____
_____
_____

Main Purpose / Main Idea
_____
_____
_____
_____

Quick summary (or abstract) of what the sources showed me and the insights I gained
_____
_____
_____
_____

Key insights and things that need to be done in society, etc. (5 or 6 bullet points)
_____
_____
_____

_____

_____

Five single annotated bibliographies (follow the form / example as listed above. Each will have several sections.

1.
2.
3.
4.
5.

Literature Review: In-Text Citations

If you plan to write the literature review essay, you will need to use in-text citations in accordance with APA style (http://www.apastyle.org/index.aspx). This page is a quick guide.

When do you use in-text citations?

Here are the places:
- Direct quotes
- Paraphrases (Please note that the APA now recommends that you include the page number as you would with a direct quote)
- Summary (not necessary to cite the page number, especially if the summary is of an entire work)

How do you refer to the author in the text?

In her description of the turtles on the beach in Lo de Marcos, Nash (2015) states that hatchlings are often eaten by predators after being released into the ocean at dusk (Nash, 2015, 12).

Hatchling turtles are often eaten by predators after they are released into the ocean at Lo de Marcos, Nayarit, Mexico (Nash, 2015, 12).

What does the final References section citation look like?

Nash, S. (2015) *Road Trip of the Mind*. Trans. Maja Kraigher. Ljubljana, Slovenia: Sodobnost.

What do you do if there are multiple authors?

Martin and Reftik (2012) pointed out that the first artists colonies new Santa Fe, New Mexico, attracted painters and writers.

What if there is no author?

Cyberbullying is considered a significant factor in teen suicide ("Cyberbullying," 2016).

Argumentation in Action: The Debate

To generate effective persuasive discourse, you must think first and foremost of the impact that your presentation will make on your audience.

If you are sitting on a stage, your presentation shared by various individuals, you are, in reality, enacting a drama. So think theater, think film, think television.

DEBATE STRUCTURE—a suggestion

Think of the debate as not only the exposition of fact and an investigative activity, but also as a persuasive discourse "in action."

Keep in mind the Pillars of Persuasion:
- Pathos—emotion (includes
- Logos—logic (includes knowledge-systems, symbol-systems, signs)
- Ethos—tone (includes the credibility, believability, and appropriateness of the speaker and/or the mode of delivery)

If you think of this as a kind of theater, or as though you were watching yourself in a kind of pageant (or as Guy DeBord puts it, as a "spectacle"), then you may have more insight on how to manage the order and presentation of the various aspects of your case.

As a presentation that revolves around the presentation of material by various individuals (actors), it is important to realize that they are, in essence, enacting roles, and the audience will respond to them in the way they have been guided or coached to respond to them. For that reason, it is vital to keep the presentation high-impact, which requires individuals to maintain separate and instantly understandable roles. The cast of characters for this particular debate can be shaped around the roles described below.

Format for Debate
The Teams
- PRO—in favor of the issue
- CON—against the issue
- MEDIA—questions both sides

The Procedure
Pre-Debate Research:
- PRO team—10 references per group
- CON team—10 references per group
- MEDIA team—5 references PRO, 5 references CON

*Include Bibliography page for our references, with 1/3-1/2 page description for each reference.

The Debate
- Opening—10 minutes
- PRO—5 minutes per person in both groups = 25 minutes
- CON—5 minutes per person in both groups = 25 minutes
- Closing—10 minutes
- Press asks questions
- 15-minute break

Each individual writes a 1-2 page response to the debate, and their final analysis of the issue after contemplating all sides, plus the press's questions

PRO team
- Position Statement (Spokesperson)
- One-sentence overview - should be direct, with lots of impact
- Three major reasons WHY this position is desirable
- Brief overview of each debate team member & presentation to the audience

Expert Testimony (Expert)
Evidence: who/what/where/why/when
- Testimonials - Emotional Appeal (The Emotor)
- Tell impassioned story
- Describe emotional impact on family, friends

- Show huge picture of victim

Community Builder: Who Benefits? Who Loses? (The Community Builder)
- Make audience members stakeholders; pull them into the community arguments
- Describe impact on community
- Show maps; before-after scenes
- Economic impact
- Crime, etc.
- Jobs & Schools

Concessions to the other side, with refutations (The Compromiser)
- Looks at opposition's points & concedes that there may be some merit
- Shows the half-truths in the opposition's assertions

Weighing the options

Summary / Conclusions (Spokeperson)

CON team
I. Position Statement
- One sentence overview
- Major emotional reason why NOT, with "evidence" support

II. Testimonial / Case Studies (The Expert)

III. Statistics (The Emotor)

IV. Alternate Community View (The Community Builder)

V. Paint scenario of what might happen if PRO wins (Expert)—Doomsday scenario (fear) (Emotor); Concedes points, but refutes them at the same time (The Compromiser)

VI. Summary / Conclusions (Spokesperson)

MEDIA team

- Question motives
- Expose underlying assumptions & demonstrate how shaky they are
- Question validity of statistics, evidence, case studies, testimonials
- Undermine biased arguments
- Impugn credibility of testimonials
- Question character of general spokesperson and/or "face" person
- Impugn credibility of the expert

CAST OF CHARACTERS

Spokesperson: Fair-minded, calm, and clearly able to communicate the primary points. This should be a person who projects a likable persona, who will make the audience feel both comfortable and confident regarding the content and the entire team.

The Expert: A serious person, "all business," who doggedly investigates statistics, facts, and figures, with a relentlessness usually reserved only for nerds and academicians. Can be slightly eccentric. Can be absent-minded, but never with respect to the numbers. Carries around piles of books, papers, reports, documents.

The Emotor: A highly sympathetic person, who fervently presents the human side of the issue, and tells a story of a person or persons who have been affected.

The Community Builder: A warm executive type, with soul. A highly connected person who sees the big picture, who works hard to bring jobs and opportunities to community members, but who can be a bit overly protective if he/she perceives that something will be harmful to the community businesses, individuals, groups, and future stakeholders.

The Compromiser: Soft-spoken, thoughtful, deliberative, willing to look at all sides, concerned with justice and ethics, then makes conclusion. Comes across as something of a worrier, perhaps too deliberative, but all the same, very credible and ethical.

POTENTIAL TOPICS

- Should our state set up workshops (participants to receive free safety glasses, respirators, equipment, etc.) in rural areas on safe handling of chemicals (avoid some of the ghastly accidents and environmental issues with do-it-yourself meth labs)?
- Should we expand the patriot act in order to put video surveillance in every home where people fit a certain profile?
- Should PetSmart set up a research center to genetically engineer animals so that they are more unique
- Do reptilian aliens exist?
- Should we put the ten commandments in every school and courthouse in the southern U.S.?

- Should we set up English-only schools and communities in the U.S.?
- Should we establish dress codes (or requiring uniforms) in college?
- Should all students be required to take a course in comparative religion (from an Islamic perspective) taught by an Imam?
- Should the U.S. eliminate the electoral college?

Capstone, Thesis, or Term Paper Guide

Sample Topic: Post-Colonial Over-Compensation in V. S. Naipaul's In a Free State, The Enigma of Arrival, and A Way In the World
http://beyondutopia.net/writing-survival-guide/thesis/

I was first drawn to the travel writing of V. S. Naipaul because his descriptions of the cultures he observed were not superficial, nor were they processed through the typical "Western filter" that typifies so many travel narratives. Instead, V. S. Naipaul approaches travel and cultural writing from a position of extreme dislocation—from his own cultural identity (an ethnic Indian born in Trinidad), from the fraying colonial geographical and "values" maps of the world, and from deep within the subsurface social machines that drive cultures, despite surface indications and official rhetoric. His characters are deeply conflicted, and they seek a place in the world. Often that requires them to create a new identity, or to refurbish their old one by realigning it with values that served well in the past. It is an interesting interplay of psychology, culture, groups, and change.

Below is one approach to a study of the work of V. S. Naipaul.

1. Abstract: One-paragraph overview, 250 words or less.

2. Introduction:

   Thesis statement—This study investigates how three of V. S. Naipaul's novels explore and offer explanations for the often vexed issues of self and society, identity, values, exile, and diaspora in the 20th century through a phenomenon that could be characterized as colonial overcompensation.

   Why the work is needed—three reasons / justifications

3. Key Terms and Definitions
   *** What is Post-Colonial Overcompensation??

Colonial psychology—identity / values / hierarchies Post-colonial holdovers—values, attitudes, internalized attitudes toward self and others
Colonialist literature
Post-colonialism
Exile VS diaspora
Social structure
Perceived hierarchy

4. Previous Work (Literature Review)—V. S. Naipaul
Primary Works
Secondary Works (by category)—about V. S. Naipaul and his writing
Other similar works—Author / Researcher / School
Other secondary works that deal with post-colonial writers / critics
(an analysis focused on critical construct or concepts)

5. Necessary Background (Bio): V. S. Naipaul

6. Historical Contexts: V. S. Naipaul and the settings and circumstances of his novels

7. Analysis of Each Work—analyzing the concept of post-colonial overcompensation to each work—each includes a) background and contexts of the work; b) themes and issues; c) prevailing critical responses; d) application to the concept of post-colonial overcompensation; e) specific examples.

    a. In a Free State
    b. The Enigma of Arrival
    c. A Way in the World

8. Meta-Analysis—toward a deeper understanding of post-colonial overcompensation as manifested in literary texts

LITERARY NARRATIVE: *Discovery Moment! Worksheet*

4 Guided Steps / Accretionary Worksheets: I've created a series of worksheets for you to follow. In it, I accompany you in responding to the guided questions, and I let you see the process of invention, discovery, analysis, and then finally, synthesis.

STEP 1: Initial Overview and Concepts

Learning objectives:
- Identify themes
- Analyze a text by reading closely and finding patterns in the use of language, the voice, and the sense of place
- Write responses to a close reading by using a worksheet
- Propose possible interpretations of a text
- Explain how the literary text relates to the reader and makes emotional connections

Jamaica Kincaid's "Girl"
http://www.saginaw-twp.k12.mi.us/view/8490.pdf

The original place of publication was *The New Yorker*, June 26, 1978.

Jamaica Kincaid's short story, "Girl" is remarkable in the way that it captures a personal voice expressed through what appears at first glance to be a stream of consciousness approach to writing. The voice is powerful and it conveys the identity of the narrator by means of a series of guidelines, reminders, and "notes to self" that show the social construction of identity, as well as the way that one defines oneself by means of daily tasks.

Because the story does not tell the reader who the narrator is, the reader may make assumptions.

There are two ways to approach this writing. Consider both, and then write a brief outline or freewrite draft that utilizes each approach.

First, one can analyze the text and point out the aspects of it that yield literary insights, both in terms of the structure and then in terms of the interpretative possibilities in the quest for meaning. Here are guiding questions to follow in your analysis:

- How does the story begin? What are the activities? What do they entail?
- Who is the narrator?
- How does the narrator express her thoughts? How does her manner of expressing the thoughts in second person impact the reader?
- How does the author use concrete descriptions and vivid details?
- Where do you find repetitions? Of activities? Of descriptions? Please list the specific examples or phrases.
- From the details provided, what can you surmise about the narrator? What does she do? What is the level of technology that surrounds her? Please list the specific examples or phrases. What might the context be, in terms of socio-economic or cultural issues?
- What are some of the values that are expressed in the passage? How do you know? Please list the specific examples or phrases.

Second, one can use Jamaica Kincaid's writing style to write one's own narrative, and then analyze it to gain insight into the way that your tasks and your social context define, constrain, and also potentially liberate you. This can be an autobiographical writing as well as a biographical or even fictive invention. I will write an autobiographical version as well as a fictive invention, just for fun.

As you reflect upon your draft and shape it into final form, please consider the following guidelines:

- Include a clear thesis statement and main idea
- Write about something that you feel passionate about
- Include at least four body paragraphs with supporting evidence
- Begin each body paragraph with a clear topic sentence that ties to the main idea / primary thesis
- Include your own ideas and relate to your own experience

Guiding Questions

Jamaica Kincaid's "Girl" Worksheet

STEP 2: Responding to the Guiding Questions

The original publication:
http://www.newyorker.com/magazine/1978/06/26/girl

In order to analyze the story, it is often a good idea to create a list of guiding questions and then systematically answer them as you refer to the text.

- **How does the story begin? What are the activities? What do they entail?**

    When I delve into the story, I find myself a bit off-balance. It's hard to tell who the narrator is, and what exactly is going on. My first impulse is to assume it's an internal monologue—one of the voices that tends to inhabit the recesses of one's mind, and which, when analyzed, tend to be a composite of the voices that we listened to and abided, which is to say we respected them to the point that we internalized them, for good or for worse.

    This voice is not a very nurturing voice, and after I read further, I see that there is a bit of "talking back" so that instead of an internal monologue, it is, at the very least, a dialogue.

The question is, "Is it internal? Or, is the voice an external one?" The next question is, "How and why might it matter?"

- **Who is the narrator?**

The narrative is speaking in second person and she is addressing the "girl" of the title.

There are at least two possibilities for the narrator: First, she could be the girl herself.

Or, second, she could be the mother of the girl.

- **How does the narrator express her thoughts? How does her manner of expressing the thoughts in second person impact the reader?**

The narrator expresses her thoughts in the form of a series of commands, practical guidance, admonitions, veiled insults, and commentary on the kind of life / context she lives in. The reader can detect a rage at the limitations of her life and also the need to conform to social norms and adhere to strictures.

- **How does the author use concrete descriptions and vivid details?**

The passage is filled with specific names and unique terms which give the text a very unique flavor; they locate it squarely within the culture of the Caribbean, without actually saying which island.

The use of idiolect for the names of music and also the names of herbs, foods, and activities clearly locate the narrative within a specific place / time / socio-economic context.

Examples:
"Wash the white clothes on Monday and put them on the stone heap"
(http://www.newyorker.com/magazine/1978/06/26/girl, 1978)

(hand-washing clothes, indicates the narrator is poor or at least that there are very basic clothes-washing techniques)

"is it true you sing benna in Sunday school?"
(benna refers a calypso-type genre, characterized by scandalous gossip—indicates the story takes place in Antigua)

"when you are growing dasheen, make sure it gets plenty of water"
(dasheen is a variant spelling of "dachine" which is the French for taro root, a starchy plant used for different dishes)

- **Where do you find repetitions? Of activities? Of descriptions? Please list the specific examples or phrases.**

There are a number of repetitions of the proper way to do household chores, but mainly the chores and tasks that a girl is expected to know

There are many repetitions of admonitions to not appear slatternly or "like the whore I know you are so bent on becoming"

- **From the details provided, what can you surmise about the narrator? What does she do? What is the level of technology that surrounds her? Please list the**

specific examples or phrases. What might the context be, in terms of socio-economic or cultural issues?

The narrator lives somewhere in the Caribbean and is very concerned about the proper way to conduct oneself in order to be respected within her society. It is not clear whether or not she is poor, working class, or middle class, but one senses that she is in a lower socio-economic level because of the number of tasks that have to be done, and there does not seem to be automation or assistance.

The narrator is female. She may be the mother of the girl. If so, she is very strict and exacting, and her admonitions are very clear. They may be done with the goal of protecting the daughter and giving her a future. However, there are so many insulting and demeaning sentences interspersed that one cannot read the passage without feeling a sense of tension and creeping despair.

If the narrator is the girl herself who has internalized the voice of the mother (or the collective consciousness of her context), it is very sad because one can see the internal landscape of repression, self-censoring, self-limitation, and above all, a profound inability to accept herself as she is.

Granted, a socialization process requires some changes to be made to oneself, but socialization processes should not require absolute extermination or extinction.

- **What are some of the values that are expressed in the passage? How do you know? Please list the specific examples or phrases.**

    This text is, in essence, a normative text.

It deals with social norms as well as family norms, particularly as they relate to the behavior and values of a young girl or an adolescent.

They are clearly sowing the seeds of rebellion, which may be healthy in its way, if it means being able to have the strength and courage to think for oneself.

However, because of the micromanaging prescriptiveness of the admonitions (After all, why wash whites on Mondays? Why not Tuesday? What are the reasons for the edicts?) and constant insinuation that there is socially reprehensible behavior just bursting to break free ("singing benna at Sunday school," walking around in a dress "with the hem coming down and .. looking like the slut I know you are so bent on becoming") or having to conceal that nature ("they won't recognize immediately the slut I have warned you against becoming"), the narrative sets up a remarkable tension. It seems to be just the narrative to function as a self-fulfilling prophecy (!)

STEP 3: Annotating my draft

Step 3: Annotating my draft

Text triggers.
More questions! Here I will add more questions and put stars & asterisks to remind myself.

I will read my thoughts and then add things to them.

It is time to engage in a dialogue with my own thoughts.

Flash connections!
I jot down the ideas, theorists, and authors whose works trigger my own thoughts.

Expandable moments!
I will mark the text when I see there is a place to expand or elaborate. How to expand? That's up to me (and my audience).

STEP 4: Clarifying the main idea & putting together an outline based on my insights

At this point, I have Step 3 in front of me, and I will start to shape and synthesize my thoughts.

The main idea I want to explore: The narrator of Jamaica Kincaid's "Girl" (1978) is ambiguous (the mother? both mother and daughter? only the daughter's interior monologue?) and the nature of the narrative illustrates psychological oppression

The sub-ideas:

** ambiguity and what it opens up in terms of interpretive possibilities and psychological processes (theoretical underpinning: Empson, 7 Types of Ambiguity)

** the dialogical imagination—what a conversation does in terms of showing norms, and also the processes that shape the sense of identity and self (theoretical underpinning: Mikhail Bakhtin / Dialogical Imagination)

** psychological oppression—what it is, how subtle it can be, and how it manifests itself (theoretical underpinning: Sandra Bartky, Psychological Oppression)

The textual support:

** descriptions of tasks

** use of idiolect (terms specific to the place)

** the nature of the admonishments

** terms used to describe the girl / female attributes and female tasks

susan smith nash

Conclusions

* Now I'm ready to flesh this out! I can mine my earlier thoughts and ideas

Jamaica Kincaid's "Girl" (1978)

The original publication:
http://www.newyorker.com/magazine/1978/06/26/girl

DISCOVERING MY THOUGHTS IN MY RESPONSES
TO THE GUIDING QUESTIONS

Now I'm going to go through my original thoughts, and I will highlight the ones that really make me think. Then, *between asterisks* I'll add more thoughts. I'll start exploring the main discoveries and the main ideas that are coming through.

- How does the story begin? What are the activities? What do they entail?

    When I delve into the story, I find myself a bit off-balance.
    **who is the narrator? a key point of ambiguity—ambiguity is one of the aspects of this work that makes it have multiple interpretive possibilities **

    It's hard to tell who the narrator is, and what exactly is going on. My first impulse is to assume it's an internal monologue—one of the voices that tends to inhabit the recesses of one's mind, and which, when analyzed, tend to be an [internal monologue that is]composite of the voices that we listened to and abided, which is to say we respected them to the point that we internalized them, for good or for not so great (!).

    flash connection! *** William Empson—Seven Types of Ambiguity http://lostritto.com/risd2013spring/wp-content/uploads/2013/04/empson.pdf

** the two possibilities: Mother? daughter? voices? ** I believe that this will be the main idea of my essay. And then I will explore the implications **

This voice is not a very nurturing voice, and after I read further, I see that there is a bit of "talking back" so that instead of an internal monologue, it is, at the very least, a dialogue.

Flash connection! Mikhail Bakhtin—The Dialogical Imagination
implications—the dialogical imagination sets up the possibility of a dialectic and it also functions as either a normative or a subversive text. It is discourse that either reinforces the norm or undermines it. Clearly, in "Girl," it does both.

The question is, "Is it internal? Or, is the voice an external one?" The next question is, "How and why might it matter?"

- Who is the narrator?

The narrative is speaking in second person and she is addressing the "girl" of the title.

There are at least two possibilities for the narrator: First, she could be the girl herself.

Or, second, she could be the mother of the girl.
**additional thoughts—what is the role of the mother? what kind of person is the mother? Here are initial thoughts—

** in the domestic sphere

*** has restricted / restrictive possibilities within her realm of influence*
*** she serves the father and the family*
*** the mother feels she must transmit values as well as "best practices"*
*** the mother instructs—but she also transmits her own rebellious attitude (via anger when listing off the rigid and restricted ways she is to do her daily tasks. She gives herself and her daughter almost no creative freedom.*
*** the mother's rigid adherence incites rebellion— probably because she herself chafes under the limitations*

- How does the narrator express her thoughts? How does her manner of expressing the thoughts in second person impact the reader?

The narrator expresses her thoughts in the form of a series of commands, practical guidance, admonitions, veiled insults, and commentary on the kind of life / context she lives in. The reader can detect a rage at the limitations of her life and also the need to conform to social norms and adhere to strictures.

** response—if this is an interior dialogue and internal voices—to repeat the litany of commands is a way of keeping the rebellious energy alive **

- How does the author use concrete descriptions and vivid details?

The passage is filled with specific names and unique terms which give the text a very unique flavor; they locate it squarely within the culture of the Caribbean, without actually saying which island.

The use of idiolect for the names of music and also the names of herbs, foods, and activities clearly locate the narrative within a specific place / time / socio-economic context.

** the words / terms seem to indicate Antigua, which makes sense because that is where the author is from **

Examples:
"Wash the white clothes on Monday and put them on the stone heap"
(http://www.newyorker.com/magazine/1978/06/26/girl, 1978)
(hand-washing clothes, indicates the narrator is poor or at least that there are very basic clothes-washing techniques)

"is it true you sing benna in Sunday school?"
(benna refers a calypso-type genre, characterized by scandalous gossip—indicates the story takes place in Antigua)

"when you are growing dasheen, make sure it gets plenty of water"
(dasheen is a variant spelling of "dachine" which is the French for taro root, a starchy plant used for different dishes)

- Where do you find repetitions? Of activities? Of descriptions? Please list the specific examples or phrases.

There are a number of repetitions of the proper way to do household chores, but mainly the chores and tasks that a girl is expected to know

There are many repetitions of admonitions to not appear slatternly or "like the whore I know you are so bent on becoming"

- From the details provided, what can you surmise about the narrator? What does she do? What is the level of technology that surrounds her? Please list the specific examples or phrases. What might the context be, in terms of socio-economic or cultural issues?

The narrator lives somewhere in the Caribbean and is very concerned about the proper way to conduct oneself in order to be respected within her society. It is not clear whether or not she is poor, working class, or middle class, but one senses that she is in a lower socio-economic level because of the number of tasks that have to be done, and there does not seem to be automation or assistance.

The narrator is female. She may be the mother of the girl. If so, she is very strict and exacting, and her admonitions are very clear. They may be done with the goal of protecting the daughter and giving her a future. However, there are so many insulting and demeaning sentences interspersed that one cannot read the passage without feeling a sense of tension and creeping despair.

*** this may be a good point of departure for a discussion of the nature of oppression—flash insights—*
*Sandra Bartky—her work on psychological oppression ** check out her essay in the Feminist Philosophy Reader (McGraw Hill, 2008), p. 51, "On Psychological Oppression" Bartky discusses how stereotypes create a psychological burden that constrains the individual, and also does violence against her by stripping her of choice, of options, and a healthy belief in herself*

https://sites.sas.upenn.edu/educationglobal/files/the_feminist_philosophy_reader_-_alison_bailey.pdf

***

If the narrator is the girl herself who has internalized the voice of the mother (or the collective consciousness of her context), it is very sad because one can see the internal landscape of repression, self-censoring, self-limitation, and above all, a profound inability to accept herself as she is.

Granted, a socialization process requires some changes to be made to oneself, but socialization processes should not require absolute extermination or extinction.

- What are some of the values that are expressed in the passage? How do you know? Please list the specific examples or phrases.

This text is, in essence, a normative text.

It deals with social norms as well as family norms, particularly as they relate to the behavior and values of a young girl or an adolescent.

They are clearly sowing the seeds of rebellion, which may be healthy in its way, if it means being able to have the strength and courage to think for oneself.

*** Question: Are restrictions and limits necessary for a healthy separation and for individuation, for the development of a separate, individual self? ***

However, because of the micromanaging prescriptiveness of the admonitions (After all, why wash whites on Mondays? Why not Tuesday? What are the reasons for the edicts?) and constant insinuation that there is socially reprehensible behavior just bursting to break free ("singing benna at Sunday school," walking around in a dress "with the hem coming down and .. looking like the slut I know you are so bent on becoming") or having to conceal that nature ("they won't recognize immediately the slut I have warned you against becoming"), the narrative sets up a remarkable tension. It seems to be just the narrative to function as a self-fulfilling prophecy (!)

As I think about shaping this into an essay—I'll definitely include more concrete descriptions

** the dress and the description of the dress
** the songs (benna)—why so provocative?
** the fear of one's own sexuality

Worksheet 2: Cultural Heritage and Human Relations

- Identify a historical / cultural place that appeals to you
- Provide background
- Describe the significance
- How does it connect to how we know ourselves?
- What is the significance for us?
- Generate a list of questions that could be contemplated
- Discuss / come to conclusions

The Wild West Show and the Ever-Changing American Identity

The Pawnee Bill Ranch and Museum has arguably the world's most comprehensive collection of Wild West Show artifacts. It was the home and ranch of Pawnee Bill, whose Wild West Shows persisted in one form or another, always bigger and better, for more than 25 years, from the late 19th century through the early 20th century.

The annual reenactment of the Pawnee Bill Wild West Show takes place each year the second week of June. It spans two days, and starts with a parade at the town square in Pawnee, Oklahoma, and ends up at the site of the Pawnee Bill Ranch, where there are permanent show grounds, as well as a museum and preserved mansion, barn, and other outbuildings. The site also contains a working ranch with American bison, horses, and cattle.

The importance of the Wild West Show as entertainment is indisputable. Wild West Shows were popular both in the major cities as well as in rural America. For the inhabitants of the urban areas, the Wild West Shows represented a dramatic spectacle that fascinated those who attended, and who held a complicated and complex notion of the American West, at once the great, vast frontier of boundless potential, while also representing the darkest recesses of the human psyche, where violence, lawlessness, unthwarted desire, and danger abounded.

If America was the place of the "Great Re-Invention" as immigrants arrived with the idea of establishing not only new prosperous lives, but also new identities, the "Wild West" was a place of absolute flux in terms of identities. It was a place where men wore hair as long as women, and ornamented themselves in silver, turquoise, and gold. It was a place where women stood on the back of horses and out-shot the men in accuracy and aplomb. It was also a place of caricatures and pernicious stereotypes, as commonly held and communicated ideas were routinely strip Native Americans, African Americans, Mexicans, Asians, and other groups of their humanity and even their lives.

The Wild West Show was, above all, a spectacle, with dramatic costumes, sharpshooting, rope tricks, stagecoach robberies, horseback football, and other events. Like a Las Vegas show a century later, the goal was to entertain the masses, and to have them arrive with dreams and stars in their eyes, all conveniently manufactured by the mass media of the day: dime novels, early moving pictures, handbills, daguerreotypes, ink prints, serialized stories in newspapers, costumes, and jewelry.

But, the question becomes, which came first: the dime novel or the Wild West Show? And, then, how did that shape the notion of American Identity?

The barrier between the two is miscible: think of the Wild West Show and the notion of American identity as fluids that constantly move back and forth, constantly mixing and changing.

Why does it matter? Here are a few implications:

* What does it mean to be American?
* What part of "Wild West" shapes current ideas of identity?
* Where and when did the exploits of the "Wild West" merge into science fiction genres?
* Where does the Wild West Show appear in science fiction movies, television, and novels?

*What are the key characteristics of Wild West personae and the dramas depicted in the enactments of the show? Here are a few initial points:

    Clash between good and evil
    Showdowns and shoot-outs (duels, updated)
    "Cowboy" values: what do you stand for if you wear the white hat?
    "Outlaw" values: what do you stand for if you wear the black hat?
    A place where anti-heroes prevail (the outsider, the outlaw, the disenfranchised, the outside-the-norm)
- Independent women (female ranchers)
- Tribes fighting to the death against the inevitable
- Counter-Christian beliefs
- The outlaw (of all kinds)
- The saloon girl / prostitute as a normalized female
- The Mexican wanderer / seeker
- The warrior who subjects himself to a "dark night of the soul"
- The vision quester
- Uncorsetted female
- The loner (often traumatized veteran)

Perhaps all these questions and ruminations would be simply a pleasing anachronism, except that the ideas persist.

While some of the stereotypes are pernicious, others are very liberating and they encourage acceptance of individual difference. Further, they are constantly in flux, and form a part of a cultural mythos that is perhaps not as well understood as we need it to be, particularly as we live in a time of instant mass communication and rapid-fire meme generation. We need to know when we're responding to an image or a set of behaviors because we've been conditioned to do so by the socialization processes embodied in cultural myth and mythos.

WRITING FOR SELF-DISCOVERY, REVISITED
Life Writing: Autobiographical Snippets (Mosaic)

Write 50–75 words that respond to the following prompts. Please select scenes or examples, and do three for each prompt. Let your thoughts flow. Do not censor yourself—simply freewrite. Use as many concrete descriptions, specific places, and vivid details as possible.

Author's note: I failed miserably in confining myself to 50–75 words! I see I need between 150–250. But, don't let my wordiness discourage you! I'm going to try this again, and see if I can keep it to 50–75 words. Minimalism.

Prompt 1: Change. *Please describe a time when you experienced a dramatic change. It could have been in your family, your place of work, school, activities, or where you lived. The change could also have had to do with changing times: technology, war, politics, economics.*

Losing My Vision: It happened quickly. In August, my father and I were challenging each other to see who could read the road signs first as we drove through the Sangre de Cristo Mountains in New Mexico. I was 9 years old, and it was a family vacation to Red River, New Mexico, where my dad undoubtedly had something geological to check out (a mine or oil wells), but my brother, sister, mother and I reveled in the A-Frame cabin we rented. The A-Frame cabin was nestled along the edge of a ridge, and a quickly flowing stream burbled along, crossable by a little wooden bridge. We spent the afternoons fishing for rainbow trout in stocked ponds, and the evenings eating them, after they were cleaned, battered in cornmeal, and fried. The colors were so vivid, the edges sharp. Then, what followed: fever and the darkened room of a weeklong battle with measles. I did not make the connection until later, but the supposedly relatively innocuous childhood disease left me with tremendously damaged eyesight. My eyesight could never be corrected back to 20/20, no matter what the prescription. I felt fragile, damaged, and unsure of my steps. I wore glasses, but my eyes would not tolerate contacts.

Oil Industry Collapse: The first time it happened, I was aware that it was probably a good thing for me. I was in my early 20s, and the early success I had in landing highly-coveted jobs and selling oil and gas prospects made me think that I was doing all those great things all by myself. The truth was, it was a great time to sell anything. Later, when oil prices collapsed, you could not give anything away. I had invested most of my profits in oil and gas leases. Unfortunately, if you don't drill a lease before it expires, it expires. That means its value goes to nothing. So, how was that good for me? I had the opportunity to diversify. I also became more resilient. Eventually.

Between Identities: I graduated with a Ph.D. in English. My Master's degree was in English as well, with an emphasis on writing. I loved avant-garde poetics, and reveled in the late 19th-century French "poetes maudits," thinking of myself as dark, brooding, apocalyptic, mystical. I would push myself into reclusive moods in order to produce edgy, intense work. But, another part of me was enterprising, creative, outward-facing, eager to make a positive mark on the world. My first job in academia required me to change. I could no longer indulge myself and plunge into the depths of my darkest "dark night of the soul." I had to change my mindset in order to survive. Sometimes, I am not sure if I really did survive—at least not my artistic side.

Prompt 2: Creativity. Please describe a time when you felt very creative. Did you express yourself creatively? Did you create something? Did you solve a pressing or pesky problem? Did you have fun, and did you feel a sense of relief?

Fishing for Hamsters: Billy Ray Cyrus, the golden hamster, had escaped from his cage. Again. I could envision him as a miniature Jaws of Life cutting off Matchbox car doors with a single snap of his mighty mandibles. In the tight utility room, Billy Ray had somehow gotten into the lint catcher part of the dryer, and I had to find a way to get him out. Crouching on top of the dryer, I slowly lowered a plastic globe I had partially filled with sunflower seeds. The twine twitched in my hands. I controlled my breath as though I were in target practice. Finally, hunger and curiosity got the best of him. He stepped into the opening where the lid once was, and entered the plastic globe, sniffing the seeds cautiously, curiously. As he filled his cheek pouches so that he looked a bit like a furry hammerhead shark, and slowly reeled in the string, lifting up the ball and its precious contents. Victory!

Prompt 3: The Unfamiliar. *Please describe a time when you were confronted by something totally unfamiliar. What was it? When did it happen? How did you feel? Who were you with?*

Lechero: When I was 18, I traveled to Bolivia to visit my friend, Violeta, who lived with her family in Santa Cruz. Almost everything was unfamiliar to me, from the way people knew who had the right of way in an intersection by who honked first, to the way people traveled from the outskirts of town to the plaza via "micros" (small vans) and "colectivos" (buses). Most unfamiliar was the way that people purchased milk: a milkman came by with a cart containing a metal tank of milk. The cart was pulled by a water buffalo or ox, guided by the "lechero" who shouted LECHE!! LEEEECHE!! to anyone within earshot. Empleadas emerged from the homes to fill their milk jugs. They would then boil the milk in order to use it. I was filled with curiosity and wonder. The way of living in Santa Cruz seemed very charming, intimate, and human to me.

Prompt 4: A Journey. *Please describe a journey that you took. It could have been a road trip, or it could have been a journey of the imagination. What did you encounter? How did you feel? What did you learn about yourself?*

Bury St. Edmunds: It's a medieval market town in East England, northeast of Cambridge and southwest of Norwich, where the female mystic and anchoress, Julian of Norwich, retreated from the world to write her *Revelations of Divine Love* in the late 1390s. I studied mysticism and Julian of Norwich, and I often wondered about the so-called "dark night of the soul" of extreme torment and feelings of despair that presage the moment of joyous reunification and illumination. I like to think of life as a mystical passage. I also loved walking around the ruins of an abbey destroyed by Henry VIII, reading the tombstones in the churchyard, and wondering if Julian had ever passed near here. If she had, she would have seen it before cruelty and a kind of cultural nihilism influenced autocrats and paranoid leaders to think that the most potent and meaning-laden fruit of human ingenuity should be destroyed, as though destroying the art would and could destroy the thought and the dream the engendered it in the first place. Live on, sweet songs of inspiration and creative courage! If I could live anywhere, I'd consider Bury St. Edmunds. But, I'd need to learn how to live with chilling winds and gray skies. I'm probably too sensitive.

Autobiographical Moments: My Leadership Moments

Write recollections that responds to "Leadership Moments" questions:

When was a moment when I needed to make a decision about a technique or technology I was not sure about? What was it? How did it turn out? What did I learn?

New Technique / Technology 1:
I was offered an opportunity to put together software training that would consist of guiding people through the software by creating a video and annotating it. There were many ways to do it—and I chose to use Camtasia. At first, I felt uncomfortable because I had used a different software, but once I got used to it, it went quite well. Later, I found I enjoyed using it.

In addition to learning the software, I learned that I can quickly adapt, and also that I can be very creative when I'm developing demonstrations.

If you don't like the Camtasia price tag (it's expensive!), I recommend Screencast-o-matic:
http://screencast-o-matic.com/home.

Here's another free software program you can use for recording videos of your desktop and including voice commentary. Webinaria is free and easy to use: http://www.webinaria.com/record.php

Prompt: When did I have to reinvent myself? How did I do it?

Almost-Disasters
It was one of those hot, humid summer mornings when the rising sun looks like a big beach ball made of orange sherbet already beginning to drip. We wanted to be onsite when they drilled through the zone of interest, and we got there right on time. It was over-pressured, but no one expected it and they had not mudded up. We drove across the cattle guard and onto the lease, and I commented that the rattling had not stopped. "Not good," said the engineer I was with. "Good time to get breakfast," he added. I looked at him, and heard shouting coming from the well. "Are you sure? " I asked. He did not answer. He was too busy turning around and backing out. We trundled on down the road, and pulled into a small crossroads diner that specialized in the kind of "comfort food" that always made me feel bloated and disgusted with myself.

The Surprising Successes
To be an explorationist, you have to be an optimist, so successes should not be a surprise. Nevertheless, the IPs of horizontal wells in the Bakken and the Eagle Ford really surprised me. In 2013, EOG filed a report with the Texas Railroad Commission that disclosed an IP of 8,650 barrels of fluid, of which 7,500 was oil. Oil was $105 and their NRI was 80%, so, assuming the production rate held up, that meant that the $6 million well paid for itself in 10 days. But at every rainbow's end is that ephemeral illusion of the pot of gold that's just over the next hill or horizon. Even without decline rates, how do you generate enough flow to pay for obtaining oil and gas leases and building infrastructure in a play that is the size of the state of Rhode Island? The surprising successes are pure oxygen pumped into board rooms and IPAA OGIS New York (Independent Petroleum Association of America – Oil and Gas Investor Showcase). The euphoria is evident in the faces of the attendees (all men, except for one lone woman) in the photo (circa 2013) on the website. I do not want to be a wet blanket. But, except for remarkable times of step-change technological change, the wet

blanket is the defense mechanism of choice to keep from making foolish choices.

Exotic Locales
If you grow up in a place, it's no longer exotic for you. So, all the residents of Baku, Azerbaijan, who looked at the vestiges of earthen pits and leaky above-ground pipelines on the edge of the Caspian Sea did not think of the location as exotic in the least. For me, however, to approach the old Soviet-era airport in the 1990s, and to see the old oil field, it was like looking at old black and white photographs of Spindletop and the Yates Field in Texas in the early 1900s. For the first time, I appreciated the environmental activists who had influenced public policy and regulations in the U.S. What made the location so exotic (at least from my perspective) was not the unfamiliarity of the geography, but the difference in mindset and historical antecedents. It made me reflect on my own values and viewpoints. I became aware of a number of flawed assumptions and prejudices that I really needed to address if I expected to benefit from the experience of being involved in a long-term project in Azerbaijan. It was life-changing, and I am grateful.

Unexpected Encounters
With snakes? Check. With gigantic tarantulas? Check. With bighorn sheep? Check. With deer and elk? Check. With scary-looking people with guns? Check. After doing field work, spending time on rigs, and holding workshops and meetings in remote locations, I developed a few aphoristic catchphrases to calm myself down. "If I make enough noise, most creatures will go the opposite direction (except for lions, bears, copperheads and black mambas)," or "Paying for equipment is better than paying for a hospital stay."

Rejecting Geology:
I think I've had to reinvent myself several times, but most recently when I purchased an older home in the tiny Oklahoma town of Pawnee, Oklahoma. I suddenly had to turn into a project manager and a diplomat but I'm not sure I did too well at either. The 1925 house I had bought at auction for $20,000 (for 2,208 square feet) basically needed everything replaced, which was a bit dismaying. What was also dismaying was realizing that I was being somewhat

gouged whenever anyone could get away with it. It got to the point where I contemplated just putting a complete halt to the entire project. There were definitely moments when I wondered if it would have been better just to sit on it without doing anything for a long time. But, that was not my overall goal. After all, I had always wanted to restore an older home, and I thought it would be fun to restore it and perhaps use it as an office or to sell it to someone who would like to use it as a bed and breakfast. After all, Pawnee, Oklahoma, is the home of the Pawnee Bill Wild West Show and Museum, and also the annual Antique Steam Engine show. There are also buffalo and the Pawnee Nation tribal center. Very interesting. At any rate, I reinvented myself as a "This Old House" remodeler. I'm still reinventing myself, and it has crossed my mind more than once that it might be useful to talk to a few contractors and put together brief videos on YouTube that help people plan their projects and thus avoid cost overruns and annoying mistakes such as ordering the wrong things.

Prompt: When was a time I overcame the discomfort I felt upon being far outside my comfort zone?

Outside My Comfort Zone 1:
Traveling for work assignments overseas has been a great way to overcome fear and discomfort due to being far outside my comfort zone. Perhaps one of the largest shocks occurred in Uzbekistan, where I was traveling to meet with government officials who were interested in obtaining technical training from the University of Oklahoma. I understood the rudiments of Russian, so the language issue was not a problem. However, meeting protocols, and the infrastructure in the old Soviet-era government buildings really surprised me. I was not used to toilets that were basically ceramic-lined holes in the floor with a pull for water to flow down and wash away the material. For the first time, I understood the meaning / origin of the term, "water closet." I also found that it was better to speak from a detailed outline than to "wing it." One morning we took a day trip to Samarqand, a gorgeous city that reminded me of what might have inspired Aladdin. It was fascinating to tour the observatory, the monument built for Timour the Great, and also the gorgeous official buildings, all constructed in the style of the "khanates." I was reminded of being in Sheki, and the similar palace in Azerbaijan, and also being in the 15th-century palace of the "Shirvan Shah" in the walled "old city" of Baku, near the Maiden Tower.

Outside My Comfort Zone 2:
When I was 22 years old, I started a small company with my dad's help. He financed my buying oil and gas leases on areas that he had long thought were very interesting and prospective for oil and gas.
I was happy to create the maps, work with the landman, negotiate with land owners, work with the trust department at the bank to buy the leases, and then to purchase them.

But, the time came to sell them! I had to line up appointments with companies and go and make presentations—in an industry dominated by males over 60! I was terrified! But, I overcame my anxiety—mainly by telling myself I could reward myself with a cute pair of shoes.

Well, after a year, I had sold two acreage blocks (prospect) and had a spectacular shoe collection.

Telling Your Story: Getting Started

The Story of Your Life

There are many reasons why the story of your life matters.

First and foremost, it's who you are, and it helps you know how you came to be who you are, with all the hopes, dreams, defeats and victories.

The more you reflect on your own story, the more you'll get to know and understand yourself, and in doing so, you'll empower yourself with self-knowledge and lessons learned.

Second, you can share your story. You'll strengthen relationships with your family, your friends, your colleagues, and your community. Sharing connects you on many different levels, and it forges bonds that are strong enough to keep you anchored during the toughest of times.

It's important to tell your story before it's too late. You can create a document that your family members and generations to come will treasure.

Finally, you can listen to the stories of others. You'll find points of connection, and you'll challenge your own beliefs and assumptions. Doors of opportunity will open – often in places you never expected.

How do you get started?

Option 1: A Chronology—a Tapestry
Think of the Bayeux Tapestry that pictorially depicted the Norman Invasion. You can tell a story through "flash images" and "flash facts" that follow the timeline of your life.

How? Here's a guide.
Write 50–75 words (or more, if you feel it's better for you) that respond to the following prompts. Please select scenes or examples,

and do one or more for each prompt. Let your thoughts flow. Do not censor yourself—simply freewrite. Use as many concrete descriptions, specific places, and vivid details as possible.

Prompts:
Birthplace – what's special about it?
Parents – key characteristics (uncensored) from your "child view" lenses
Hometown – what makes it unique?
School – memorable event
Memorable class
Memorable out of school activity
Awkward moment after I graduated
Love & heartbreak
Early employment
Better employment & why / where
My changing goals
Family as it is now

Where do you store your ideas?
What kinds of sources do you have?

Telling the Story of Your Life

Option 1: A Chronology—a Tapestry
Think of the Bayeux Tapestry that pictorially depicted the Norman Invasion. You can tell a story through "flash images" and "flash facts" that follow the timeline of your life.

How? Here's a guide.
Write 50–75 words (or more, if you feel it's better for you) that respond to the following prompts. Please select scenes or examples, and do one or more for each prompt. Let your thoughts flow. Do not censor yourself–simply freewrite. Use as many concrete descriptions, specific places, and vivid details as possible.

Prompts:
Birthplace – what's special about it?
I was born in Ardmore, Oklahoma. During its 150-year life, it has been a frontier railroad town, an outlaw hideout, the world's largest inland cotton port, Oklahoma's largest oil producing town, the site of Oklahoma's worst plane crash (killing 83 people), and the birthplace of several Fortune 500 companies. Imagine. All that, and still at this point Ardmore is small. It has only 25,000 inhabitants.

Parents – key characteristics (uncensored) from your "child view" lenses
My dad traveled to exotic locations, from oil and gas wells to mining prospects in the American West. His travels fascinated me. My mother loved to create things—dollhouses, crafts, beading, painting, and more. It was a kind of parallel play, that I'm just now able to appreciate.

Hometown – what makes it unique?
I consider my hometown to be Norman, Oklahoma, since that is where I grew up. What makes it unique? Almost everyone would say that it's the University of Oklahoma. I'd agree, and would add that having all the sports and arts facilities also available to local residents made it an amazing place for a child.

School – memorable event
I was always recognized for my musical abilities: piano and violin. They were very gratifying, and the music teacher, Mrs. Crow, would often ask me to perform for the class. I loved it.

Memorable class
Skip to high school. By far my favorite class was English Literature. It opened my eyes in many ways, and my teacher, Mrs. Bailey, was a retired pharmacist who had sold her store after her husband's death, and had moved to Norman to live with her mother. I rode my bicycle during blistering hot summer days to visit her and her mother, and to talk about literature.

Memorable out of school activity
When I was 16, my piano teacher challenged me to give a performance of my repertoire. That meant playing at least 10 pieces by memory, for a performance of more than 2 hours. It was terrifying – something like preparing for a tennis match or swim meet. I practiced sometimes up to 4 hours per day. The evening came and I did well. Later, though, I never wanted to do anything like that again. It was a good exercise, but it cured me of thinking I'd like a career in music. I did not like performing enough to shape a life around it.

Awkward moment after I graduated from high school
I fractured a bone in my foot while wearing high-heeled platform sandals on the first day of the fall semester my freshman year at the University of Oklahoma. The orthopedic surgeon was a total heartthrob, and I fantasized about his asking me out for a Coke. So, when it came time to have my knee-length cast removed, I dressed in a cute miniskirt, and wondered about where we might go for a Coke. Things did not go as hoped. The first thing that the doctor said to me was, "Hey, it looks like you've only got one shoe and sock. Hope you brought one." Oops! So much for impressing him! He cut off the cast, and I was horrified to see a leg that was as furry as a polar bear. I did not know whether or not to take off my one shoe and sock and to go barefoot, or to try to angle myself so that people would not see the furry leg and grubby foot. I could hear him chuckling to himself as I hobbled out, one bare foot, and one nicely

shod with knee sock and funky mini-platform oxford. Once outside, I stuck my hairy leg in the bushes next to the sidewalk as I waited for my mother to pick me up. Disaster!

Love & heartbreak
I fell hopelessly in love with my guitar teacher the summer after my freshman year in college. He had a guitar studio across the hall from my dad's office, and he intrigued me. He was 26 or 27 and I was 19. His name was "Ogden" and he said everyone called him "Dogden" when he was a chubby, sweaty kid. I thought he was extremely cool, and I liked accompanying him on the piano as he riffed and improvised in flamenco-esque excursions a la Al DiMeola or Paco de Lucia. I even joined him on a weird liquid protein diet to the point of gauntness, while he puffed up like a marshmallow roasting over a fire. He never even gave me a hug, so I finally faced the fact that he was not interested in me. My sacrifices were not worth it. I listened to Dan Fogelberg and Julio Iglesias and sobbed alone in my room. Life was not fair.

Early employment
One of my first jobs was at the University of Oklahoma where I worked in the College of Pharmacy's library. I enjoyed reading about the new products and the case studies. It was in the same building as the anatomy lab, which I came to understand contained cadavers. Later, I worked in the College of Engineering as a summer engineering student in the area of membrane ultrafiltration. I received the Outstanding Freshman in Chemical Engineering award, and had the idea of going into bio-engineering.

Better employment & why / where
One of my favorite summer jobs while I was an undergraduate was in Cape Girardeau, Missouri. I worked as a summer engineer at the Proctor & Gamble paper products plant where they manufactured disposable diapers (Pampers and Luvs), and Rely tampons. I was assigned to the tampon factory. My project for the summer was to determine the viability of substituting 4-ply for 5-ply strings, and maintaining the same strength and effectiveness. My studies demonstrated it was possible, and I was offered a job the next year. It was a great experience.

My evolving goals
My dad said he thought that engineering was not a good path to follow. All the really wealthy people he knew were geologists. I think he was biased, since he himself was a petroleum geologist. I could not seem to overcome my fears of failure in engineering, so I followed his advice. I graduated with a degree in petroleum geology at the height of the boom, which meant I got to experience the full extent of the crash. As a result, my goals changed, and I focused on other areas. I've made so many changes, and have had so many decision points and forks in the road that it's hard not to ask myself "what if…"

Option 2: A Free-Form Mosaic Built on Themes

Think of colorful mosaics made up of pieces both large and small. Create "flash memories" around themes and put them in any order that makes sense to you (even random). You'll be amazed at how the juxtaposition of disparate parts will trigger your mind to make connections. It will be a surprisingly generative and revelatory experience once you've got the pieces in place.

How? Here's a guide.

Write 50–75 words (or more, if you feel it's better for you) that respond to the following prompts. Please select scenes or examples, and do one or more for each prompt. Let your thoughts flow. Do not censor yourself–simply freewrite. Use as many concrete descriptions, specific places, and vivid details as possible.

Prompt 1: Change. *Please describe a time when you experienced a dramatic change. It could have been in your family, your place of work, school, activities, or where you lived. The change could also have had to do with changing times: technology, war, politics, economics.*

Prompt 2: Creativity. *Please describe a time when you felt very creative. Did you express yourself creatively? Did you create something? Did you solve a pressing or pesky problem? Did you have fun, and did you feel a sense of relief?*

Prompt 3: The Unfamiliar. *Please describe a time when you were confronted by something totally unfamiliar. What was it? When did it happen? How did you feel? Who were you with?*

Prompt 4: A Journey. *Please describe a journey that you took. It could have been a road trip, or it could have been a journey of the imagination. What did you encounter? How did you feel? What did you learn about yourself?*

Prompt: Creativity

I've had to be creative many times in my life in order to reinvent myself. It's been a good thing. However, sometimes I think of creativity as something focused on problem-solving, and that might actually limit me. Can we be creative just simply for the joy of it? For the artistic self-expression?

I'd like to find creative alternatives for things that bother me, and thus solve animal cruelty, and also cruelty to those who think / feel / behave outside the norms.

EXAMPLE
The Unfamiliar: Oklahoma Oktoberfest

I have only a vague idea of how or why Oktoberfest originated, and the first thing that comes to mind is a large log building with split log tables where men in lederhosen drink from gallon-sized frothy mugs served by blonde women in low-cut embroidered blouses and full skirts somewhere in the mysterious reaches of the Black Forest.

I'm assuming Oktoberfest originated as a harvest festival and was motivated by the desire to celebrate that, thanks to work, teamwork, plenty of rain, no root rot or infestations of plant-eating pests, there would be no mass starvation this year, during this years' during the long, dark, cold winter.

That's not really a reason to celebrate Oktoberfest in Tulsa, Oklahoma, which abounds with Wal-Marts, Whole Foods, and a number of local supermarket and convenience store chains (Reasors, QuikTrip, Kum-N-Go come to mind), all of which are very effective purveyors of provisions to paying customers and also the local food pantries.

But, the advent of temperate weather and balmy evenings just before we go into the dark nights of the soul provoked by Central Standard Time most certainly qualifies, at least in my mind.

I first became aware of Tulsa's Oktoberfest when what seemed to be hyperanimated Country & Polka penetrated my 14th floor condominium. It was not something that motivated me to embrace the event. In fact, I contemplated writing a letter complaining about the noise pollution at 11 pm on a weekday night. I spend enough time championing the futile and the self-serving, so decided against it. Instead, I stood on my balcony and looked across the Arkansas River to the west side, just south of the 11th Street bridge. I watched the neon-bright Ferris Wheel and other rides on the Midway and wondered how many children were losing their bratwurst, funnel cakes, and Slurpees in a dark corner that someone (like myself) would inadvertently tread upon.

Last year, the day after the final day of the Oktoberfest was warm and cloudless, and a perfect day for taking a walk along the RiverParks bike and pedestrian pathway, which took me to the grassy spaces used for setting up the booths, stands, tents and rides. I could not really tell what had gone on in the tents; they were already deserted and awaiting decommissioning by efficient crews zipping around in forklifts small pickup trucks.

There was definitely evidence of convivial embibing; empty beer cans and an empty plastic bottle of something emblazoned with a dancing demon and a label that stated "Fireball: Cinnamon Whiskey" which I assumed was cheap enough to appeal to the crowd that would actually appreciate the cheapest, sweetest, strongest alcohol available. I suspect that the good old university stand-by, Everclear, must have fallen out of favor. Too much trouble to mix with something, I guess.

The beer cans and empty Fireball bottles reinforced the impression that I had that the main purpose of Oktoberfest was gluttony: drink as much beer as possible and gorge oneself on greasy snacks. It seemed all the world like the State Fair, minus crafts and animals.

But, the weather was glorious, the air clear, and the sense of coming together to spend time with one's friends and family, and to build experiences and memories, suddenly seemed more clear. People want to spend time together, and they enjoy focused, destination-driven activities. At least that's what I'm able to glean from the proliferation of tailgate parties, State Fair events, and festivals, the quirkier the better.

I'm actually a fan of quirky festivals, and have been to the Rush Springs Watermelon Festival and various other local ones, including Noble's Rose Rock Festival.

I've talked a good game about wanting to go to the various Rattlesnake Roundups in Oklahoma, but when push comes to shove, I recoil and start thinking it's really cruel, even if there is an overpopulation of rattlesnakes, and even if they need the snakes for their venom (to synthesize anti-venom). It reminds me of the time I attended a bullfight in the little Jalisco town, San Miguel Los Altos, for their patron saint day the 29th of September. This was far from the kind of tourist town where you'd see a lot of influence from U.S. tourists and stakeholders, and so it was not Disneyfied in the least. The six bulls that took part (and were killed, of course), were dispatched with varying levels of skill and artistry. In one case, the artistry was so misdirected it turned in to butchery. I was rooting for the bull. Perhaps it would have a chance to maim or gore its picadors and matadors: it's not that you can fight the inevitable, but at least you can show a bit of fight and spirit as you face your destiny. That's all in theory, of course. You don't really know how you'll respond, and the U.S. presidential candidate who commented on the passivity of the victims of (yet another) mass shooting in a school, and said that he would never just stand there, he'd resist, probably deserved the vociferous social media shellacking he received from the relatives of the victims.

Back at the bullfight and five or six street dances to brass bands and mariachis later, when the friend I was with introduced me around town as his wife, I did not know how to take it. It was amusing, but I also found myself feeling alternatively annoyed and mildly outraged. I've analyzed that reaction many times, and I'm still not sure I understand all the contributing factors to my response. Partly, I felt I was being mocked as a blonde American and the only American tourist I saw that entire evening. The other was the assumption that he was some sort of prize that I'd just love to be considered his wife, even if it was just for some bizarre motives of his own. I always circle back to the fact that there must be some tremendous cultural gulf, even if I do speak, read, write, and understand Spanish. It's time to reread Octavio Paz's *The Labyrinth of Solitude*, I suspect.

Oktoberfest is probably one of the more faithful cultural appropriations we have from our patchwork overlay of immigrant cultures. What is intriguing, even charming, from a cultural anthropologist's point of view is just how creating a spectacle that has as its first purpose to engage people, and to allow them to perceive that the experience they are creating is memorable and gives meaning to their lives and their relationships, does so by providing a flexible framework that opens itself to new additions to the ever-increasing constellation of "traditions" (something that has been done at least once can qualify as a "tradition," I believe.)

I'm all for unifying festivals and the evolution of socially constructed traditions.

Prompt: Freewrite

FREEWRITE #1
MCCLENDON'S WAKE

Sui generis. Yes, that's how it is, and that's the only way to break through in a lifetime of striving; if you don't make it by the time you're 35, you're not really likely to have a team, a company, or an entire concept named after you. But you risk vilification. Oh yes, that's the risk. Bracket your life around the needs you placed in a basket behind you. Oh yes, it's the way we break the tiles, seek the mosaics; up and down the staircase, the Great Chain of Being. My sister said she smelled a demon in my father's house. Sulfur and roses. I think that's the level of hydrogen sulfide that's supposed to kill you instantly. Sour gas. Very sour. Ventura Canyon-level sour. Don't make me remember. But still, I like those flows of memory – like the down-filled comforter I put on my bed, the duvees I switched out every week. I love the variety. I'm not the kind to leave a duvee in Mexican beach town where it will mildew within a week, and where I get sick every other time I visit, although I rarely get sick at home or when I travel. Let's go with the rainbow. It's something we need to paint in sugared, flavored, carbonated water, and not with water vapor & light. Oh yes, it's what we say is "unreadable" but it really means "undrinkable." Water of light, water of life. I remember what I don't want to remember, and pull back into my heart of hearts. I loved those lunches together. Long, with laughter. But you could never be the person who could really commit, and I felt shivering and humiliated. Blasted into a bridge, foot pushing the accelerator all the way to the floor. I'm starting with you in a way you can understand. Sure, it's all one paragraph, and certainly it's a bit dense. But, you can at least accept it's easy to read. The syntax is simple. The words are smooth. The sentences convey meaning. But as a whole, the meaning splinters because it's not at all a single, coherent conceptual block. I must continue to charge ahead. Walk, walk, walk on my way from West Junior High School, my platform wedgies the coolest I had ever seen, ordered from a catalogue with hundreds of shoe designs to choose from. 15 years old. Long legs made longer with 4 inch platforms. Guys used to honk and shout at me as I walked home. I look back and wonder what they were thinking. Nature's green is golden. That's all I can say. I loved the 30-minute walk home. I stopped by 7-11 to buy a few snack items to tide me over and then I would think about what I wanted to be, do, feel, experience in the future. Oh what a future! Immersion in a place that was kinder, deeper, more beautiful. It's not very fulfilling to have to constantly tell yourself you don't really care that he does not call, does not seem to care. Even though you know you are the one who ran away, and you know he has to protect himself somehow. Aren't you tired of playing it so you can have it both ways? You think you're winning; you think you're in control, but that false thinking just brings you farther down the road to what will necessarily be a disappointing end. I'd like this to be as unreadable and I am not sure what it means – moldy, fragile papers? Or, defenseless

FREE WRITE #2
DECEMBER OAKS

I was listening to the radio and thinking of redemption. You were on my mind as the salt water closed over my head and the ocean kicks up dandy and turbulent.

Salvation is blue like circling thoughts. I always see the same things on this stretch of road.

A black Jeep. A white pickup. Rows and rows of oak trees that still have your leave although it is December. Oak trees are a strange breed or species. They have leaves that they do not like to share. So oak trees will share their leaves in a windstorm throughout the winter, not just in the fall without first grace and hard hit freezing breeze and yes, how unwelcome it is.

Unwelcome ice.

The way that leaders intercalate with pine and oak make a mosaic after earth fish up towards the sky. The Browns the rusty greens and the then Great Basin tween the lives. Between the limbs.

Do I have to shout to be understood?

The truck were unpredictable in the deepest part of night and in the whole-swallowed past.

We were talking about politicians and presidents. You said you read that politicians after they were out of office became solitary loners. I have a difficulty believing that. To me, a politician is a gregarious animal who needs constant affirmation and also needs to heal as his persuasive power. I can't imagine a politician as a loaner. I don't even really think of politicians is being fingered although it is true that thinkers have gone into politics. There has been philosophers and writers who have become politicians.

The politician flash president role is a different one. Especially if they are creative writers the politician who is also a creative writer is interesting. I am trying to think of a few and I cannot think of many Americans who were creative writers and presidents of the of the nation. However, in Venezuela there was Romulo Gallegos Gallegos. And in Peru there was Mario Vargas Llosa Mario Vargas ll OSA.

The president who were writers also wrote in French and thinking of Aime Cesaire is there also if I was correct and I think a couple of Caribbeans were also writers. It would be good to have an intellectual as a president, I think. Now that are you select no I'm not sure. Is it good to have a utopian as a president? And if he is such a thinker will his utopia necessarily be someone else's dystopia? I think the answer to that is yes. Yes.

EXAMPLE: JOURNEY
CITY DIFFERENT: SANTA FE, NEW MEXICO

I'm not sure what to think of a place that seems so light-drenched and enchanting one day, then shadowed with mystery and history the next. It's not the first time this has happened to me in Santa Fe, New Mexico. It seems to happen to me each time I visit, and it always takes me by surprise.

I

Santa Fe, New Mexico, was first settled in 1598 and became the principal city for a large region belonging to the Spain. It was important as a center of commerce, culture and general adjudication. Later, after Mexican Independence, the Mexican-American War, and more, it became a territory of the United States. It was important as a part of the Santa Fe Trail and center of commerce, but it is far from the mining towns of Colorado, and also far from secure sources of water. The system of managing irrigation ditches (sequias) worked for centuries, and water rights were critical for ranching and sheep-raising. But, things declined, and in the late 1800s, visitors commented that it would be hard to imagine a more dismal place than Santa Fe; the people who lived there subsisted on little more than red chilies, onions, and mutton.

Sometime around the construction of the railroad and some sort of expansion, wealthy city dwellers discovered Santa Fe, and it became something of an artist colony. Visionary planners determined a "City Different" concept, and decreed that all buildings had to maintain architectural consistency, which included adobe and brick, with an emphasis on incorporating native flora, including cottonwood trees, mesquite, sage, and lupine. Pueblo Indians along with the various other tribes in the area contributed culturally unique weaving, beadwork, rugs, pottery, and more.

II

The result is a charming admixture of influences from Pueblo Indians, colonial Spanish, Mexican, and Old West / cowboy culture, and it feels a lot like an illustration from a 1890s Western dime novel.

That's the part that always charms me. The first day, walking around, feeling the light breeze, the warm air, the smell of sage and mesquite, never fails to captivate me and make me think of myself in the U.S., circa 1910, with a magical sense of expansiveness and freedom.

But, something happens. I'm now convinced it must be physical, but I'm not sure what. In my ramblings, I start to feel the thin, dry air's impact on my skin, and my face starts to feel like a crumpling piece of paper, and the exclusive art galleries and purveyors of artisan items start to seem to fall into mysterious shadows.

Ceramics galleries that should, by rights, appeal to retirees and vacationers who would like to decorate their own ceramics, are filled with hand-painted and fired mugs, plates, and vases. They are quaint, and their Grandma Moses primitivism is charming, but their price tags are not: $120 for a mug; $75 for a plate. I suppose that one could consider them to be collectables, but the quirky DIY (do-it-yourself) and vintage-cowboy vibe is eroded. I can't imagine why the workshop does not let people have classes and then potentially sell stuff on consignment in a gift store.

On Guadelupe Avenue, the oldest sanctuary Virgin of Guadelupe is a lovely mission-style church. Unfortunately, it's locked. The statue outside, which is wreathed with with bouquets of flowers, is serene and calming. Across the street, Mexican men gather to seek work for the day. I suppose they're paid cash and under the table. It's a hard life.

III
My sister believes there are restless spirits in New Mexico. I have to say that it could make sense if it is arising from a violated earth and environment. It's one of those dark edges, a "resource curse"—in

Grants, lots of uranium ore, and then, north of Santa Fe in Los Alamos, figuring out what to do with it. We all know the story. Today, the Albuquerque baseball team is named the Albuquerque Isotopes.

For me, Santa Fe offers an icy plunge into wish fulfillment.

Do you think you like nature? A laid-back Bohemian life? Time to write, sculpt, paint? Welcome to Santa Fe. What happens to the flash drives you fill with digital manuscripts? What happens to the canvases stacked unframed in your garage studio? Or the shelves of painted ceramic mugs, plates, bowls? What happens to your weavings, embroidered pillowcases, cross-stitched guest towels?

The future is unknowable. The midnight-blue shadows behind the pale yellow cottonwood leaves suggest that the present is likewise so.

Do you want to grab onto the American Dream? In the park across the street from the oldest sanctuary (still locked) in the United States for the Virgin of Guadelupe, the group of Mexican men seeking work has swelled to 40 or 50.

"I'm lost," I say in Spanish. "I just arrived, and I'm looking for downtown."

It's a weak conversational gambit, but it works. I manage to have a nice conversation with a small group, and I learn that work is scarce, and they're worried about having enough earnings to eat and to pay rent. I thank them for their efforts and tell them I admire their drive and hard work. Several thank me for speaking in Spanish, and I apologize for my accent. I suppose that having an Oklahoma accent makes it clearer that learning Spanish has been a matter of choice, of passion, and of years of dedication (although I've been intermittently dilatory, which I attribute to the fact I have not had the opportunity to travel very extensively, or to live in a Spanish-speaking country.) Plus, although one might not believe it to see me now, I'm a bit shy about talking to people.

I wander around the church and try to find an open door. All are locked. I encounter younger males—probably around 18 or 20. They are thin, appear to have a very hard life. One comes up to me later and speaks to me in a combination of Spanish and English, and tells me that he has just washed his shirt. Now he is hungry. I do not know quite what to say to that. His friend talks about the importance of having a stick and a blanket. I think the younger one has probably huffed a lot of glue in his life. Tears come to my eyes. I chat a bit. I do not have any money with me so cannot help them. I'm reminded of the homeless who spend time on the banks of the Arkansas River in Tulsa. They make quite a contrast to the Mexicans across the street who, on the whole, exude a much more positive "can do" attitude. I realize that with these homeless adolescent males, tragic stories abound. It is heart-rending.

IV

It's close to 11 a.m. I'm feeling a deep gnawing that is partially hunger (I have only had water so far today) but the feeling also has something else. I slept rather late, lost in a world of disturbing dreams and persona from my past and in different time periods.

I want to explore the depths of the shadows behind the leaves. I am fascinated by this place. Its beauty, pungent aroma, and the quality of light seduce me within the first few minutes of arriving. But, almost as quickly, I'm forced to listen to questions I can't block or eliminate from the voice in my head. What is happiness? That one is too cliché, and it is too easily silenced with endorphins from exercise or a high-pressure presentation. The dark, hard questions are the ones that creep in around the edges of consciousness. What happens when the things you've been working toward all your life turn out to be trivial and/or meaningless, or, you're simply not very good and your output is worse than forgettable, it's awkward and embarrassing? What do you do when, compelled by a sense of duty, you assume family roles that are extremely destructive? How and why does every goal or desire seem to contain built-in contradictions?

I look at the clock and am secretly relieved that I will need to head to the airport in a few hours. I can flee the light and the thin air before I've had to really probe my inner thoughts, and to hash over the same old turf of self-analysis. If I stayed for a few weeks or a month, perhaps I'd be able to work through the archeoliths of my unconscious. I must leave, and so will not have time to do so. I have the option to continue to resist change and true transformation.

V

Perhaps I'm not quite ready to confront my own depths. Perhaps transformation still gives me pause. Although I do not like to think so, transformation can cut both ways. Instead of ascending to a higher level of consciousness, I can always sink into an abyss; mire myself in a Slough of Despond of my own making.

In my heart of hearts, though, I do not want to stay at the same point. I want to journey between the inner and outer worlds, and I perceive Santa Fe as precisely the place that opens dimensions.

I contemplate a cottonwood branch with its light yellow leaves glistening in the pale yellow light. I see the shadows dancing on the cool white trunk of the tree.

I am ready.

BOOM AND BUST

West Texas crude lost 71 percent of its value since June
Someone stole the pumping units from our lease
Floodwater breached our earthen dam
And yesterday a travel trailer burst into flames

The copse of cedars immolated themselves in sympathy

I don't know where you end, or where I begin
I don't know where I end, or where you begin

Drill unity into the heartbeat
Spill experience onto the floor
Clouds sag into the horizon
Scissor-tailed flycatchers line up on high-tension wires
Risking heart,
       risking flying too high,
              risking irregularities of mind,
                    of rituals of Being

And you and I
We risk memory and simple atonement
For the things that might have been
The perfect pairings when prices were high
A stocked farm pond
       with all the requisite cottonmouths
             and adrenaline surges

Two souls united by rupture
Boomtimes & going their separate ways

We cross Oklahoma's own Bridges of Sighs
I carve dice from some unnamed set of bones
You mow down poison sumac
     with the AK-47
          I told you to never buy
Minnows fall from sky

QuikTrip cappuccino coagulates in my cup

I miss you already
Although you're at my side
My hand is warm; the wind is cold
Yes, you bring the heart
      The abandon
           The first and last memories
                  Staining like this Oklahoma blood-red clay
                  Oxygenated both hopeful and hopeless
                      And still we believe…

APPENDIX: EXAMPLE OF A RESEARCH PAPER IN PROGRESS

The "Honor Killing" of Social Media Star Qandeel Baloch: Technological Change, the Changing Roles of Women, and Grassroots Backlash

Abstract

The murder of Qandeel Baloch was just one of hundreds of "honor killings" that take place in Pakistan every year. However, because she was an outspoken social media star with more than 700,000 followers, her death brought attention to how social media has brought new focus to the evolving roles of women, has resulted in a grassroots backlash. At the same time, an examination of the specific accomplishments of Qandeel Baloch provide insight into a deeply and fascinatingly subversive artist who essentially invented herself, appropriating the tools and techniques of Western media sensations, and subsuming them in her own context(s). Further, an evaluation of what occurs in so-called "honor killings" makes it clear that "honor cultures" and violence toward women are universal, and the lessons learned in the death of Qandeel apply across the board, globally.

Introduction

"Oddly enough, those are two things that Pakistan does not deal with well: the Internet and "badly behaved women"
—Masterjee Bumbu

The outspoken model and social media celebrity Qandeel Baloch was killed by her brother on July 15, 2016, at her family's home in Multan, Pakistan. The murder was an "honor killing" and it was a response to what her brother perceived as a loss of family honor due to the racy photos and videos, and her poses with a Muslim cleric where she donned his signature cap that she posted and disseminated through YouTube, Twitter, and Facebook, where she had more than 700,000 followers, which was a staggering number, given that she primarily spoke in Urdu, which necessarily limited her reach.

Her brother, Waseem Azeem, was arrested a day later, and stated that while his sister (born Fauzia Azeem) provided resources, he found her behavior humiliating for the entire family. In an interview with the Associated Press, he said he could not endure what people were saying to him, and he had decided to either kill himself or her. (CBS News, http://www.cbsnews.com/news/qandeel-baloch-brother-pakistan-murdered-honor-facebook-photos/)

"Money matters, but family honor is more important," explained Azeem (CBSNews.com) as he described how he administered sedatives and then suffocated her in her sleep. Their father, however, expressed outrage that his son murdered his own sister (regardless of "honor"), and rejected the notion that he would seek clemency.

Clearly, he considered it his duty to kill the errant family member who had taken several pages from the Kardashian playbook to "break" the Internet with provocative, openly sensual messages and videos. She also spoke out against Pakistan's patriarchal society and was an advocate for "girl power."

Honor Killings in Pakistan: Background and Contexts

Make no mistake. Pakistan does not condone honor killing, and Azeem will be charged with murder. According to changes in the law, unlike in the past, now in an honor killing, the family does not have the right to pardon him.

Nor does the church condone in any way honor killings. In fact, in June 2016, the Council of Islamic Ideology (CII) restated the position it took in 1999 that honor killings are un-Islamic (BBC, 2016). The statement against honor killings followed a May 2016 release which expressed the position that it was permissible to engage in the "light beating" of women, which the Human Rights

Commission of Pakistan immediately condemned as "ridiculous" (HRCP, 2016).

The HRCP, which maintains statistics on different types of human rights violations maintains a separate category entitled "Honour Crimes" and it covers both men and women. Between January 1 and July 15, 2016, at least 262 women were killed in an "honor killing." Of those, at least 44 were minors (hrcpmonitor.org, 2016).

The most prevalent reasons for the honor killing were illicit relations and marriage choice. Most of the suspected killers immediately went on the run, although some were apprehended into custody and a few surrendered voluntarily.

According to the HRCP, honor killings are on the rise in Pakistan, although it is difficult to determine to a precise degree, since many go unreported and occur in rural areas. The statistics that are gathered are based on monitoring reports in 15 newspapers and news websites, and reports from HRCP volunteers (hrcpmonitor.org, 2016).

Why are honor killings on the rise? There are many suggestions.

What Did Qandeel Do?

When Waasem Azeem was arrested, he expressed pride that he had killed his sister because she was bringing dishonor to the family by her scandalous poses in social media, which included a series of scandalous poses with a high-ranking cleric, an offer to do a strip-tease for the Pakistani cricket team, a video in which she danced to a song warning her that she would be banned if she continued to move her hips the way she did, and increasingly political statements chiding officials and championing the rights of women.

Qandeel's presence was epitomized by a sense of humor, self-parody, and willingness to say outrageous things in order to get attention. In one of her most outrageous acts, she met with the Mufti Abdul Qavi, whose views on women were very conservative. Her selfies with him give a very compromising appearance as he appears to shed layers of clothing (in one photo, he's wearing a waistcoat and cap, and in another, he is waistcoat-less and capless). Qandeel poses wearing his signature cap. For Western readers, Qandeel's approach was playfully subversive. For world readers, she was alternatingly titillating, entertaining, liberating, and enraging. For her family, her behavior was scandalizing, even though her work as a model was the main source of income for them. An overview of Qandeel Baloch's life and impact appears on her Facebook page: https://www.facebook.com/OfficialQandeelBaloch/videos/876282005849886/

Perhaps Qandeel thought she would, Samson-like, topple pillars of the religious structures of the society as she interviewed a religious leader. She was a critic of patriarchy that often oppresses women. However, the interview was sufficiently scandalous that the powerful religious (and political) leader was suspended from his post. Qandeel did openly challenge the conservative culture and mindset around her and she invented and re-invented herself.

In a July 4, 2016 post on her Facebook account, Baloch wrote:

> Atleast international media can see what i am upto. How i am trying to change the typical orthodox mindset of people who don't wanna come out of their shells of false beliefs and old practices.
> Here this one is for those people only.
> Thankyou my believers and supporters for understanding the message i try to convey through my bold posts and videos. It's time to bring a change because the world is changing. let's open our minds and live in present.
> #QandeelBaloch #TheSensation #BBC #BBCUK #Podcast

Under the post, she posted a video that explored her persona and image:
https://www.facebook.com/OfficialQandeelBaloch/videos/876282005849886/

She thought of herself as a feminist, and in doing so, she followed in very auspicious footprints, including among many others, the ideas in such works as Mary Wollstonecraft (1759-1797) *A Vindication of the Rights of Women* (1792), John Stuart Mill's *The Subjugation of Women* (1869), and Sor Juana Ines de la Cruz's "Respuesta a Sor Filotea de la Cruz" (1691) in which Sor Juana defends women's right to knowledge.

In the 21st century communications technology milieu of the U.S., it's a bit hard to imagine that an Internet sensation could be capable of doing anything overtly politically shocking, particularly since it's the goal of social media and reality television to provoke a response. In fact, people will go to amazing extremes to go viral—even if what they are doing is self-destructive, reckless, or just plain ridiculous.

While it is tempting to look at Qandeel as rather derivative or imitative, the way that she appropriated social media, and both subverted and worked within the social media discursive framework, is worth noting.

From a somewhat different perspective, Qandeel's accomplishments included the following:

1. Intimacy that achieved remarkable levels, especially difficult to accomplish in a "nothing's private" world of the Internet. She posted videos on YouTube that showed extreme vulnerability and a need for approval (manifesting as a need to be found attractive), while inventing herself and a persona that is brash, outspoken, and calculated to both repel and attract the viewers in the very conservative Pakistan.

Love her or revile her, you could not stop watching. The reason was not because of Qandeel's singing or dancing talent, nor her beauty, but because she triggered an emotional response. Audiences confronted their own beliefs, and also found themselves (even some of their secret desires) reflected in a mirror that showed more than people wanted it to show.

2. Enacting and making visible the dynamic that usually stays invisible. Behind extreme enthusiasm for sports is a complex mélange of emotions in the fans. First, there is shared pride and projected identity. But, second, are emotions connected to flow, vitality, urge, and finally, sexuality. In the U.S., it is not uncommon to hear of female fans flinging themselves at famous athletes. The fact that athleticism connects to an eternal spring of reproduction is something usually veiled. But, not for Qandeel. Hence, the offer to strip for the Pakistani cricket team if they won their match in the World Cup, and when they lost to India, she performed a highly sensual dance for the Indian team.

3. Reinventing herself after marriage / motherhood. Her Internet name, Qandeel Blaloch, was not the one she was born with, nor was it her husband's name. Fauzia Azeem reinvented herself as Qandeel Blaloch, the provocative yet vulnerable self-actualizing, reifying selfie (and extended selfie) as well as the playful presence who liked to poke pins into the puffed up cultural authorities. She poked a pin in them, but they did not pop immediately, but you could see the air starting to go out of them. An example was her selfie video with the mufti Abdul Qavi as she spent time with him breaking the fast in the hotel room where he was staying. It is not clear why they met, but she did at one point claim he was in love with her. Whether or not that was true is not clear. She also proposed to a cricket player on the national team who refused to even meet her in person. (https://www.youtube.com/watch?v=vJkm3flB46g)

It is worth noting that the individuals who had the real last name of Baloch had sued Qandeel for defiling their surname. Her brother listed the fact she had besmirched their name as one of his justifications.

4. Appropriation and reinvention of American pop culture. We tend to think that Americans appropriate other cultures, both as a melting pot, and as a commodification of anything that moves. We forget that cultural appropriation cuts both ways.

Qandil take twerking and makes it her own. Twerking and other dance moves have been around for a long time, first in R&B / rap, and later in crossover acts such as Miley Cyrus's performances. It is customary to think of a global cultural colonialization via art and music, but Qandeel (and others) show an appropriation of, among other things, twerking, and making it completely her own. She does not have to get naked (Miley Cyrus) or engage in hyperactive choreographed frenetic sweating (no end to these!), but instead melds influences and makes the moves her own. They are, as in her other videos, remarkably touching—perhaps because you see vulnerability and humor in the performance, and not simply raw libido.

In a television talk show in Pakistan, Qandeel is asked to dance, and her choreography, while labeled as "vulgar" by some, brings together traditional Pakistani dance with other influences. Again, she makes it her own.
http://www.dailymotion.com/video/x3fywjm

In "Ban," which was published just 8 days before her death, Qandeel weaves in a variety of dance forms (twerking among them), and subsumes all within a Punjab narrative (https://youtu.be/PtD72-js8dQ) (I'm using the narrative to refer to discourse).

In a heartbeat, libido slipped into thanatos, and Qandeel is now the embodiment of the chiaroscuro, life-death dialectic one finds in the most enduring works of literature and art, including *Othello, Romeo and Juliet, Tristan and Isolde,* and others.

5. **Toying with and taunting an important and respected person in the church and government.** Qandeel like playing with fire. It is one thing to twerk and talk about stripping for a team while you're videoing selfies from your bed. It's another thing to orchestrate a series of selfies and a selfie-video that gives the impression that the religious leader has violated the most basic tenets of his own religion (fasting, abstinence, prayer, respect) to the point that he is stripped of his position, authority, and prestige.

Ambition and the pursuit of her goals impacted others, and resulted in collateral damage. Here we tread in uncharted territory. In fact, Qandeel's brother said the selfies with the mufti provoked him into resolutely deciding to murder his sister, and presumably restore the family's honor.

Nowhere does the Koran condone what he did, and if he did actually manage to restore the family's honor by murdering someone for behaving badly, it was an illusion, and would only appear to be the case because of misinterpretation and a kind of collective social delusion about the law and the church's edicts.

Honor Culture, Honor Killings

The usual knee-jerk reaction to the killing of someone who has been offensive or somehow transgressive usually involves condemning the entire culture, wholesale. Certainly, the murder of people who annoy, shock, scandalize, or deliver unpopular messages can never be condoned.

But, it's more complex than that, and we certainly can't throw stones when our own culture has its own severe ways of dealing with individuals who transgress social norms. Sex and sexuality may no longer be the "hot button" but certainly the perceived attempt to humiliate or cause harm can result in catastrophic reprisals.

1. **Men are victims, too, in honor cultures.**
While brothers or fathers who conduct the "honor killing" may claim to feel they did what they had to do to defend the honor of their family, there must be a psychological toll. To feel compelled to kill someone is painful, and it brings to mind the honor cultures of the past, where duels were obligatory if one's honor was besmirched.

In the statistics maintained by the Human Rights Commission of Pakistan, the number of men murdered or victims of "honor killings" is lower than that of women, but men are killed. The reasons most cited were for marrying against the family's wishes and for behavior outside marriage.

Most cultures seem to pass through an "honor culture" phase, and in doing so, there are severe limitations to personal autonomy and self-determination.

2. Can you culturally quarantine your black sheep?

There are awkward tensions between individual and collective identity. In a culture that focuses on the individual and individual accomplishment, if a family member misbehaves, then a great effort is made to distance them and say that each person is responsible for their own choices. Rehab it is. Or, exile. The individual is quarantined, in essence, and it is not necessary to kill them to eliminate their threat, although it may be necessary to train family members to stop feeding the black sheep.

3. What is "honor" in times of rapid social change?

In a collectivist, "high context" culture such as that of Pakistan, individual identity and reputation are often linked to a group affiliation, which can be a tribe, family, political unit, or community.

In the traditional Punjab culture, gender roles are very clearly defined, and the family unit survived by careful resource management. Marriage is a business and political union, and the man and wife are expected to respect each other, and potentially grow to love each other. Romantic love has no place in the marriage, which was traditionally arranged as a negotiation between families.

Any family member who does not behave in accordance with social norms runs the risk of damaging the family honor, which in turn determines the survivability of the entire family. The worst situation is for the family to lose honor, and thus lose the ability to maintain one's position in society, one's livelihood, and general survivability.

In times of rapid social change, the rules and limitations that once constrained people's lives often loosen, and with education, communication, and a global framework, it's possible to find employment and livelihood in the new world order. As a result, women can (and do) find independent means of funding themselves and their families. Sometimes (as in the case of Qandeel), the methods are completely at odds with the old social order.

Institutions (church, government, workplace) evolve with the changing times, but they tend to be a step behind, except in cases of totalitarian autocracy, when the populace is catapulted into modernity, such as in the case of Kamal Ataturk in early 20th-century Turkey.

The murder of the woman who represents change is also an attempt on the part of the murderer to nullify changes. His actions represent the extreme position of the person who craves the social order of the past where he occupied (or at least thought himself capable of occupying) a position of prestige. More than a nostalgic longing for what is past, the "honor killing" represents a violent rejection, and on some level, a sickeningly satisfying rage for order.

To the man who murders for "honor," the reality he cannot face is a world where honor means nothing, and honor gets you nowhere. Instead, shock, shame and transgression are the new tickets to fame and glory.

Conclusion: The Lesson Is Universal

I have found myself questioning whether or not I should write about this topic since I do not live in Pakistan and I do not have first-hand knowledge of the social context.

However, honor killings as such do occur outside Pakistan; according to statistics, they also occur in India, Afghanistan, Turkey, and in the U.S. and the U.K.

And, once we accept that an "honor killing" is nothing more than a rationalizing label affixed to murder, the case becomes very clear. Murder of "badly-behaved" women happens quite frequently in many different cultures.

Here are a few thoughts about "honor killings" and the murder of women who make people feel uncomfortable.

1. Technology-driven social change can have unexpected consequences. Technology that accelerates societal change seems to always come with an evolution of the social order, whether it be the family structure, the government, the institutions, or all of the above.

In the case of technology, it often expands the opportunities for individuals to be independent, and the education that is necessary has the effect of opening many doors.

Women and the traditionally powerless suddenly have the ability to choose the direction for their own lives, with an unprecedented level of self-determination. There is a new sense of liberty.

But, there is often a tug of war between "liberty" and "libertinism"—and those who use their liberty to become libertines often fall apart in self-destruction and dissolution.

Further, a culture that privileges "libertinism" over true "liberty" may move from a manufacturing or agricultural base to one that emphasizes entertainment. The issue is one that seems to accompany rapid social and political change. For example, Elizabeth Gaskell (1810-1865) explores in *My Lady Ludlow* (1858) the difference between liberty and libertinism in the changes following the French Revolution.

Many critics of a consumer culture have pointed to the commodification of the female body to simply accelerate the pace of consumption of ephemeral goods or activities. The woman who is able to shape her own role as a model and to self-promote can, in theory, empower herself. However, the capitalist structure that makes it possible still remains outside the body of the woman being used. So, like it or not, she is simply being used (while she is young) to sell products (or to be a product herself).

The first tragedy is that Qandeel Baloch was murdered because she was inconvenient for someone else.

The second tragedy is that Qandeel Baloch never really transcended the fact that others were using her body for their own purposes. Perhaps it was not for producing children or tending to family members in the traditional conservative role, but her "liberty" played into the libertine desires of a consumer culture, and she was complicit in her own commodification.

If she had lived longer, perhaps she could have built her own advertising agency or her own product line. Then she could have had one foot in each economic modality: manufacturing and entertainment.

At any rate, the question to be asked is, for the young woman aspiring to be a success in a celebrity culture, and who wishes to use the means at her disposal (social media) to achieve that goal, what is the end game? For the one who wants to create her own celebrity (rather than facilitating the celebrity of another), what is the actual trajectory of likely outcomes, especially given that celebrity is often fleeting, and for those who managed to make themselves (like zombies or other undead) unkillable (like Madonna), we are faced with watching a spectacle we no longer enjoy except as it produces memories for us, like a step into a time machine.

The irony is that in death Qandeel is more commodifiable than ever, and she is likely to achieve more sales / attention than she ever did or could have in life.

Her instant martyrdom makes the tragedy of her brother's life-ending (for his own life as well) doubly painful. He killed her to "defend the family's honor" (and ostensibly expunge her bad behavior and artifacts and restore the family to their pristine, unstained condition) and yet more people than ever will see her. He said he would either kill himself or kill her. He did both.

2. Violence against women occurs across the globe. There may not be as many honor killings in Western countries, potentially because we live in a less collectivist culture, and the individual is considered to be responsible for his or her own reputation. "Family honor" does not seem to matter too much except in political dynasties or small towns. The black sheep would be sent to rehab or to the big city. Then, if they're financially successful, all they have to do is build a mansion, drive expensive cars, and start donating to foundations.

Even if there are not honor killings, violence against women is on the rise. Women are sexually, physically, and psychologically savaged at work and at home. Intimate partner violence is a significant problem. According to the Center for Disease Control (CDC), once every 20 minutes an intimate partner is the victim of violence in the United States (CDC, 2014).

There are many reasons for intimate partner violence. Much has to do with poor stress and anger management. However, more than anything is the reality is that it is a social phenomenon and a learned behavior, and underlying collective beliefs and attitudes about women perpetuate / promulgate the behaviors. Further, the problem is compounded when the individual starts to internalize the negative psychological impacts, and starts to believe they deserve the bad behavior, or that it is somehow the norm and inevitable.

Honor killings in Pakistan and intimate partner violence in the United States probably have more in common than they have differences. And, so, we can learn from each, and possibly start to work with the vectors of socialization (institutions such as families, communities, churches, schools) to internalize unconditional respect, as well as stress and anger management techniques that actually work.

****

REFERENCES

Oddly enough, those are two things that Pakistan does not deal with well: the Internet and "badly behaved women."
—Masterjee Bumbu

BC. (2016). Pakistan 'honour' killing: Why clerics' call may fall on deaf ears. 15 June 2016. http://www.bbc.co.uk/news/amp/world-asia-36542285

BBC.com (2016) Qandeel Baloch: Pakistan social media celebrity 'killed by brother' / July 16, 2016

CBSNews.com (2016) Brother admits murdering model sister of "honor" lost to Facebook pics. CBSNews.com 17 July 2016 http://www.cbsnews.com/news/qandeel-baloch-brother-pakistan-murdered-honor-facebook-photos/

DailyBhaskar.com (2016) "Pakistan Got its own Poonam Pandey! Here's What She'll Do If Pak Wins WC '16" http://daily.bhaskar.com/news-hf/TOP-world-cup-t20-pakistan-vs-india-model-offers-to-strip-for-shahid-afridi-5276572-PHO.html?seq=4
http://www.bbc.com/news/world-asia-36814258

Human Rights Commission of Pakistan (HRCP) (2016) "HRCP condemns 'ridiculous' CII recommendations. HRCP.com 27 May 2016 http://hrcp-web.org/hrcpweb/hrcp-condemns-ridiculous-cii-recommendations/

Human Rights Commission of Pakistan (HRCP). (2016). Honour Crimes (Women/Men) http://hrcpmonitor.org/search/?id=5 accessed 17 July 2016.

PT (Pakistan Times) (2016) Qandeel Baloch claims Mufti Qavi 'hopelessly in love' with her! June 20, 2016
http://www.pakistantoday.com.pk/2016/06/20/news/mufti-qavi-breaks-fast-with-qandeel-baloch/
Qandeel Baloch / Aryan Khan (2016) "Ban" Beyond Records.
https://youtu.be/PtD72-js8dQ

Sharma, Aditya. (2016) Qandeel Baloch Murder: Honour Killing Plagues Pakistan. Over 1000 Cases Reported in 2015. http://www.india.com/news/world/qandeel-baloch-murder-honour-killing-plagues-pakistan-over-1000-cases-reported-in-2015-1336559/ July 16, 2016.

Zee Media Bureau (2016). Pakistani internet sensation Qandeel Baloch stirs controversy by clicking selfie with Mufti Abdul Qavi 23 June 2016. http://zeenews.india.com/news/south-asia/pakistani-internet-sensation-qandeel-baloch-stirs-controversy-by-clicking-selfie-with-mufti-abdul-qavi_1898890.html

About the Author

Dr. Nash earned her Master's and Ph.D. in English at the University of Oklahoma, where her emphasis was on discourse analysis. Her Bachelor of Science degree in petroleum geology is from the University of Oklahoma. Since graduating, Dr. Nash has studied graduate-level economics with an emphasis in developmental economics, and has earned certification in instructional design from Texas A&M and Florida State College Jacksonville. Her books on writing and learning, *Writing for Human Relations* and *E-Learning Survival Guide* have had more than 75,000 downloads.

www.ingramcontent.com/pod-product-compliance
Lightning Source LLC
Chambersburg PA
CBHW030140170426
43199CB00008B/145